# ONCE BLIND

*The life of*

## JOHN NEWTON

# ONCE BLIND

## The life of

# JOHN NEWTON

### KAY MARSHALL STROM

**Authentic**

COLORADO SPRINGS · MILTON KEYNES · HYDERABAD

Authentic Publishing
We welcome your questions and comments.

USA     1820 Jet Stream Drive, Colorado Springs, CO 80921
        www.authenticbooks.com
UK      9 Holdom Avenue, Bletchley, Milton Keynes, Bucks, MK1 1QR
        www.authenticmedia.co.uk
India   Logos Bhavan, Medchal Road, Jeedimetla Village, Secunderabad
        500 055, A.P.

Once Blind
ISBN-13: 978-1-934068-27-4
ISBN-10: 1-934068-27-6

12 11 10 09 08 / 8 7 6 5 4 3 2

Published in 2008 by Authentic

Scripture quotations are taken from the authorized King James Version. Public domain.

Library of Congress Cataloging-in-Publication Data

Strom, Kay Marshall, 1943-
  Once blind : the life of John Newton / Kay Marshall Strom.
    p. cm.
  ISBN-13: 978-1-934068-27-4
  ISBN-10: 1-934068-27-6
  1. Newton, John, 1725-1807. 2. Church of England--Clergy--Biography. 3. Hymn
writers--England--Biography. I. Title.

  BX5199.N55S773 2007
  283.092--dc22
  [B]
                        2007041662

Cover Image: "A Liverpool Slave Ship" by W. Jackson © National Muesum Liverpool,
Merseyside Maritime Museum

Cover design: Paul Lewis
Interior design: Angela Lewis
Editorial team: KJ Larson, Betsy Weinrich

Printed in the United States of America

# Contents

# CHAPTER 1

# 1790

DONNED IN A FRESHLY POWDERED WIG AND CRISP CLERICAL ROBE, Reverend John Newton stood in the pulpit of London's stately St. Mary Woolnoth Church. He looked old. Old and profoundly weary. Still, since precious few seafaring men survived to see the age of sixty-five, who could say whether it was his years that wore on him or just this day?

Wealthy tradesmen and upper-class businessmen, accompanied by their exquisitely dressed families, had arrived early, and with much fanfare, settled themselves in the forward pews— *their* pews. Further back, the "ordinary folk" squeezed in close together . . . shopkeepers and laborers and widows and such—the people the reverend held particularly close to his heart. Visitors packed in behind and between and around the regulars, and spilled out into the aisles and entryways. They came from all over London . . . indeed, from across England, and even as far away as Scotland. Every Sunday was the same when John Newton was in the pulpit.

Reverend Newton leaned forward, squinting to make out the individual faces of his flock. It was no use. The people he had grown to love so dearly appeared as little more than a collective blur. His eyes, always weak, had grown so dim he could barely read his sermon notes. Just as well, perhaps. This might not be the day to see faces clearly.

"You know me for what I am," Reverend Newton began. "Not a person of mighty consequence . . . only a great sinner saved by God's grace."

Rustling in the pews. Eyebrows raised and glances exchanged. Whispers.

"Some of you are aware of the fact that a Slavery Abolition Bill has been sent to Parliament," the reverend continued. "As I have intimate knowledge of the slave trade, my dear William Wilberforce has requested my testimony before a select parliamentary committee. I consider myself bound in conscience to answer this call . . . to wash my hands of the guilt which threatens to constitute a national sin, stained with crimson dye."

The rustling stopped and whispers ceased. Silence fell over St. Mary's. It was almost as if the cathedral itself was holding its breath.

With the slightest tremor of weariness, Reverend Newton continued: "Since I agreed to appear, I have received repeated threats from some who benefit most by the cursed trade. They say that if I insist on going through with my testimony, they will reveal to you, my dear parishioners and friends, the darkest evils of my own wretched past life. I will be publicly shamed and humiliated. Even forced from the ministry. They accuse me of being a hypocrite. Well, my friends, I can only say that I hope it will always be a subject of humiliating reflection to me that I was once an instrument in this awful business at which my heart now shudders."

An uneasy shuffling among those in the forward pews.

"Every age seems to have people who have made a habit of evil, who have had to look up in order to see the bottom," said Reverend Newton. "Yet in the day of God's power, they are saved and transformed. They become an example to other believers, giving them an opportunity to praise God for his amazing grace. I, my good people, was one of these. God saved me so that people would look at me and say, 'If God could save John Newton, he can save anyone.' Surely you can understand, then, that my silence at such a time as this would be criminal . . . even though my words come too late to prevent or repair the misery and horror to which I was an accessory."

Many of those crowded into the church that morning owed their livelihoods—indeed, some great fortunes—to the slave trade. Of this fact, John Newton was well aware. Besides, these people worshipped in a respected cathedral of the Church of England, not in a meetinghouse of Quakers or, even worse, of Dissenters. Not in the expected haunts of evangelical rabble-rousers.

"Those of you who have read my publication, *Narrative,* must think you know me well. But had I given details of the wickedness of my heart and life, it would have been too shocking for my readers to bear."

As Reverend Newton's passion grew, a new strength and authority overtook him. His weariness fell off like a worn-out cloak.

"No, my dear friends!" he exclaimed. "You will not hear it from them! You will hear it from me. I will tell you my story. . . ."

# CHAPTER 2

# 1736

*"I was born in London on the 24ᵗʰ of July, 1725. My pious mother dedicated me to God when I was still an infant. With no brothers or sisters, and my father away at sea for years at a time, I enjoyed the full attention of my mother.*

*She was my teacher, my playmate, and my friend. There was no place I would rather be than by her side. But, alas, my peaceful and happy childhood was short-lived. By the time I was eleven, I was already at sea."*

"ALL HANDS ON DECK!" BELLOWED THE FIRST MATE. "TO YOUR stations!"

As thunder rumbled, wave after wave slammed against the ship's creaking timbers. Lifted high on the back of a swelling surge, the ship seemed to soar, only to suddenly pitch forward into darkness.

"Father!" cried a small, shaky voice.

Eleven-year-old John Newton pushed further into the tiny space between a large barrel and a stack of crates stuffed with frantically clucking chickens. But the howling winds and crashing waves swept his terrified cries away.

For over a year John had begged his father to bring him along to sea. He didn't care about the length of the voyage, he insisted.

Comfort didn't matter. He just wanted to escape the detestable boarding school . . . and to be with his father.

Finally his father had consented. But for what? To let him drown in the sea?

"Father!" John screamed frantically. "Father, help me! I can't swim!"

The ship lurched, sending the chicken crates tumbling and John sliding across the water-slick deck. Sobbing and clawing, John managed to grab hold of the shrouds and cling to them until the ship stopped rocking. Then, hunkering on his knees, he clasped his hands together and squeezed his eyes shut. "Help me, God!" he cried. "Save me! Please, please . . . stop this storm and save me!"

The wind's howling quieted to blustery billows. Crashing waves calmed. And all around the kneeling boy, sailors paused to breathe a collective sigh of relief.

Leaning back on his heels, John wiped his sleeve across his tear-streaked face. Then a shadow fell over him. Straight and stiff, without so much as a wrinkle in his uniform, Captain John Newton, Master of the Vessel, loomed over his son.

"F-F-Father," John stammered as he scrambled to his feet and quickly came to attention. "Sir! I was so afraid. I—"

"In my quarters," his father ordered. "Immediately."

✦

For what seemed hours, John stood at attention while Captain Newton paced, back and forth, back and forth. From the door, past the desk, to the leather arm chair: twelve paces. Sharp turn, back past the desk and all the way to the door (thirteen paces counting the turn). Back and forth, back and forth. John fixed his eyes on the intricately carved mahogany desk that filled most of the room.

*Why had his father chosen such a huge piece of furniture for so small a cabin?* John wondered. On top was a large sheath of maps and a magnifying glass to read the small print. A white ivory dragon on one corner and an elephant carved out of black wood on another. Ebony, his father had told him. That was the black wood. From Africa. John didn't know where he got the dragon. In their London house every table in every corner held something from his father's travels: pictures, carvings, silk pillows . . . even a toy boat. John wasn't allowed to touch them, of course, not even the boat. But he could look at them.

Back and forth, his father paced, back and forth, back and forth. Then, two paces past the desk, Captain Newton abruptly stopped and swung an about-face. John trembled, his lips quivering.

"My own son!" Captain Newton pronounced each word as though it was bitter in his mouth. "Crying and blubbering in front of everyone, and all because of a little storm!"

John knew better than to try to defend himself. Stand quietly at attention; that was the proper response. He knew it. Yet he still blurted, "But . . . I was so scared. . . ."

"You . . . embarrassed . . . me!"

*Be quiet, John. . . .* He knew. *Let it go. . . .* Never argue with his father. *Take your punishment. . . .* But the words tumbled out in spite of himself.

"I didn't see you anywhere, Father. I thought—"

The captain's stony control burst into rage. "Sailors don't think! They act! Everyone on that ship was doing his job. Everyone except you—my own son!"

Hot tears flooded John's eyes and spilled down his cheeks. Quickly he swiped at them with his fists and gulped back his sobs.

"Your mother made a baby of you! Well, starting today, that will change."

John squeezed his eyes tight and willed himself back to the peaceful days at home in London. Just him and his mother and no one else. Reading together and learning Latin . . . singing songs . . . playing games and laughing. . . .

"John! John, are you listening to me?"

John forced himself back to attention.

"You *will* grow up!" his father ordered. "You *will* be a man!"

"Yes, Sir!" John replied.

"Now, to the galley with you."

"Yes, Sir."

The galley! If his father wanted him to be a man, why not order him into the rigging? Why not out on the yards? Why not all the way up to the topmast? (After some practice, of course.) All alone in the crow's nest, sitting at the top of the world. . . . That's where John longed to be. But, no. It had to be the galley. . . .

✦

" 'Bout time yer draggin' yersef in 'ere," Cook groused when John arrived. "Well, git to the fire."

Far from the peace and tranquility of the topmast, John set to work in the cramped galley, bent over the bubbling caldron of steaming stew.

"And don't ye be lettin' it burn," Cook warned. "Else I'll take me spoon to yer backside till ye . . . !" Cook's potential punishment was drowned out by his debilitating cough that started with a deep rumble and ended up leaving him struggling for breath.

Whenever Cook coughed, John quaked. It sounded dreadfully like his mother's cough. Cook slumped forward, clutching his chest, and John shook so badly he slopped stew out onto the flames.

*Don't make me remember!*

His beautiful mother, so sweet and frail, coughing, coughing, coughing . . . finally took to her bed and stayed there day and night. . . . Her friend Elizabeth came to visit, but when she saw his mother she wailed out loud. Before John knew what was happening, Elizabeth bundled his mother up and rushed her to a waiting carriage. No time for a kiss goodbye, or even a pat on the cheek. As the carriage rumbled down the cobblestone street, John ran after it screaming, "Wait! Wait for me!" But a neighbor lady grabbed him and held him tight, and the carriage disappeared into the fog. Night after night he had prayed that his mother would return. Day after day he had watched for the carriage to clatter back across London Bridge. Then one day the neighbor lady said, "She isn't coming back, lad. She's dead and gone to heaven."

Thirteen days later John turned seven years old. But his childhood was over.

"'Ere now! Stop snivelin' into me stew!" Cook ordered. "Ye want me tellin' yer Pap ye was blubberin' like a baby again?"

No. No, John definitely did not want that.

"Them men isn't waitin' all day fer the food," Cook said. "'Urry now!"

In his struggle to hoist the heavy pot off the fire, John managed to slosh still more boiling stew, this time right onto his hand.

"Oowwww!" John cried. As he jumped back, he let loose of the pot. Just in time, Cook's calloused grip caught the handle.

"If ye isn't the most useless—"

Cursing John soundly, Cook carried the pot to the table. "Git the biscuits, then!" he called over his shoulder. "Kin ye at least git that right?"

*No,* John thought. *No, I can't do anything right.*

That's what Tomasin, his father's new wife, had told him.

Being a ship's captain in the Mediterranean trade for the East

India Company, his father was away at sea when Elizabeth Newton died—just as he was away at sea when John entered the world and for most of his son's life. How John had longed for him to come home and make everything all right. But when his father finally did return, he very quickly introduced that new wife who had her own way of doing things. She didn't like the London house, so they moved to her father's farm in Essex. Away from everything John had ever known and loved . . . away from Dr. David Jennings' Dissenter church where people knew him and cared about him and remembered his mother . . . away from the only things John had ever known: learning and reading and singing hymns and reciting scripture. Never in his life had he played with other children. In Essex, John didn't fit in.

"Go outside and play with the other boys," Tomasin ordered. But when he did, she scolded him for the bad habits he picked up from "those wild and ill-mannered ruffians" and for copying their coarse talk. "You have never even been to school!" she complained. Yet she had no interest in reading with him or listening to him recite his Latin. As for his father . . . well, he had no time for a sad young boy.

"Git along with yer chores!" Cook ordered, and John shook away the memories. Goats and pigs and sheep in cages below deck, kept for fresh meat during the voyage, were his responsibility. Which meant food, water, and clean cages every day. The chickens in the crates on the deck—he cared for them, too. When Cook turned his attention to the oven, John snatched a biscuit off the table. But before he could pop it into his mouth, Cook's heavy spoon cracked him across the head.

*Nothing changes. Land or sea, it's all the same.*

When John started getting into trouble, Tomasin insisted he go away to boarding school. John begged to study at home, but of course his father took Tomasin's side. So John was added to the clutch of boys who lived and studied at a local schoolmaster's house. Aggressive and exceedingly harsh, the schoolmaster handled every disobedience—even the most minor—with a crack from his cane. He took an instant dislike to mild-mannered John, and he absolutely terrified the lad. When he stood over John and bellowed questions, the boy did his best to stammer out an answer. But *Crack!* the cane invariably came down on him. Before long, John found it impossible to choke out even the easiest answers. "Dolt!" the schoolmaster had roared. And as the other boys smirked and jeered, blow after blow rained down on John's aching shoulders.

"Men's done eatin'," Cook announced. "Git something fer y'self, then clean up." By the time John had scrubbed up—including the bulkheads and the deck—the ship's bell was sounding middle watch—midnight. As silently as possible, he edged into his father's cabin. Although the light had already been doused for the night, the room was so small John could feel his way to his cot without disturbing his father. John stretched out his aching body, but despite his weariness, sleep evaded him. With every wave that thumped against the hull, the ship's timbers groaned. His father turned over in his bunk, then resumed his deep-sleep breathing. John reached up and gently touched the sagging bulk that was his straight, at-attention father. So close yet so far away.

From John's earliest memories, he knew better than to speak first without asking his father's permission. Or to sit before his father sat first. John was well-acquainted with the consequences of failing to stand at attention when his father entered the room. After his mother died, John lived with neighbors for almost an entire year waiting for his father to return from the sea, only to have him bring Tomasin. Still, John had tried to cling to him. But then baby William was born. And the strict, distant captain suddenly changed into a Papa who rocked the baby, and played with him, and . . . well . . . *loved* him. John was an outsider peeking in through the window at a family he didn't even know.

"Please, Father," John had implored. "Take me to sea with you. Teach me to be a ship's captain just like you. Please, Father!"

John slept in his father's cabin, and he ate at his father's table. But that's where his privileges ended. If anything, Captain Newton maintained a stricter list of rules for young John than for the other sailors. And whenever he and his father stopped in port, his father strolled through the sellers' stalls searching out gifts for baby William. Or maybe for Tomasin. But never for John.

During that first voyage, John did move from the galley to the rigging. During the second, he learned to stand under the billowing sails and call sheets. And although his father sternly forbade it, he looked the other way when John eased out along the high yards, then slid down the mizzen stay.

Despite stretches of time in Essex, John eagerly looked forward to the next order to weigh anchor.

"Be tough!" his father ordered. "Be tough or you won't last."

CHAPTER 3

# 1740

*"I was religious in my own eyes, but, alas! There was no foundation so it passed away like a morning cloud. I learned to curse and blaspheme, and I was exceedingly wicked. . . . I saw religion as a way of escaping hell; but I loved sin, and was unwilling to forsake it."*

"AH, LONDON! IT TRULY IS THE GREATEST CITY IN THE WORLD," CAPTAIN Newton sighed as he slammed the carriage door and settled back on the leather seat.

"If you like smoke from a hundred chimney stacks belching smoke into the air," John said. "And the stink of too many people crowded together with their horses and chickens and—"

"Ha!" his father snorted. "You go on a few sea voyages and you think you know everything. Look at those modern houses. Brick and stone, not wood that dries into tinder. And nicely paved cobblestone streets. My father told me plenty about old London before the great fire cleared out all the rat-infested tenements."

But John was no longer listening. It wasn't in London that he spent his time between voyages. Soon the broad, congested roadway of the bustling city would narrow into a country lane and they would be on their way to Essex where he could do as he pleased. Out with the lads who had taught him the fine art of snitching from marketplace stalls. Who had helped him develop his colorful vocabulary of swear words. Who had trained him to stand up to anyone who tried to boss him—an art he practiced at home when his father wasn't around, and more brazenly aboard ship behind his father's back.

"John," Captain Newton began, "whether you go to church or not makes no difference to me. But with children in our house, and Tomasin, too, I do expect you to mind your behavior. Especially your mouth."

Scowling, John turned his face to the window. Criticize and scold! Criticize and scold! That's all he ever heard from his father. Grow up, he said. Well, every sailor on the ship cursed, and the great captain didn't correct them. And who was his father to be lecturing, anyway? His religious efforts were laughable. On Sundays, he pompously marched out on deck and forced the crew to listen to perfunctory reading from the *Book of Common Prayer*. Boring! No wonder the crew snickered and mocked him.

Now John—at least he was sincere. After his first ocean voyage, he came back to Essex to find the other boys in awe of him. Amazing! He spun tales of his adventures—more than a little exaggerated—and they begged for more. Soon he was strutting around, bragging about his exploits and his prowess. He jumped up on a horse and raced the others across a meadow. But that devil of a horse threw him over its head, and he landed beside a row of sharpened sticks in a newly cut hedge. Mere inches from certain death! All John could think was, *What if those stakes had run me through, and right now I was standing before God?* Quaking with terror, John vowed to change his life. No more swearing. Prayer every day. Scripture, too. And not just reading it, but *studying,* too . . . making notes in a journal. Of course, that vow had only lasted a month or two, but still. . . .

". . . because when I was your age I had completed my schooling by Jesuits where I learned discipline. . . ."

John didn't even pretend to listen to his father's tiresome lecture. Soon he would be rounding up his friends, the wildest lads in the countryside. They would all expect grand tales from him, and John would see that they got them.

To John's great pride, he could out-boast, out-lie, and out-curse every one of the lads, and he grabbed every opportunity to prove it. One day a fellow named Thomas announced, "A warship's moored up the Thames. Sure would be grand to see it!"

John boasted, "I could get us a guided tour." Thomas was duly impressed, so John said, "Meet me at the riverbank forenoon tomorrow, and I'll get us over on the tender boat."

John's plan was to arrive early and fast talk his way in. But when Tomasin's father registered yet another complaint about the boy's laziness, Captain Newton insisted John do his part of the chores. When he finally managed to slip away, John set off for the Thames at a fast trot, cursing his father the entire way. He arrived at the riverbank just as the tender boat pulled away from shore.

"A lad named Thomas," John asked. "Anyone see him?"

"Aye, 'e was on the boat," an old man said. "'im an' a passel o' lads with 'im. All braggin' about seeing the warship, they was. And askin' after a John Newton."

Fury exploded inside John. His &*%$ friends had no right to sail without him! And if it weren't for his *&%! father, he wouldn't have been late and missed the %*& boat. As John stood on the bank fuming and cursing, the waters turned rough, churning and tossing the tender boat. Suddenly a wave slammed against the side, flopping it upside down. John froze in shock as terrified screams echoed over the water. Cries of horror rose up from the bank and joined the wails of despair.

No one survived.

"I was supposed to be with them," John gasped. "Just five minutes earlier. . . ."

As John made his way home, his mind a jumble of terrified thoughts, it suddenly occurred to him, *"God protected me!"* The hand of God, just as Reverend Jennings preached at the Dissenter meetinghouse on Gravel Lane. John had enjoyed attending there with his mother because the sermons were not nearly as boring. The people talked about God in an entirely different way. And they sang hymns. Almost unconsciously, John hummed a favorite of his and his mother's . . . then he sang Isaac Watts' words out loud:

> When I survey the wondrous cross,
> On which the prince of glory died.
> My richest gain I count but loss,
> And pour contempt on all my pride.

Two days later, John stood by Thomas' graveside. No more bragging and boasting. No cursing or blaspheming. John could only think, *God protected me for some reason.*

Although it seemed a lesson seared forever into his memory, soon it too began to fade. By the time the command came to weigh anchor for the next voyage, the whole event was all but forgotten.

Fifteen-year-old John's work-hardened body was not all that toughened up at sea. Both his tongue, sharp and cutting, and his troublesome attitude quickly turned the other sailors against him.

"John," Captain Newton said after they finished eating and the other officers had left. "I have been thinking about your future." He picked up his china cup and slowly sipped his evening tea. "And I must tell you, I'm not certain a life at sea is right for you."

"What! You *&^#@—"

Captain Newton slammed his cup onto the table. "Stop it!" he ordered. "I will not listen to such talk! In a fortnight, we are due to drop anchor in Alicant, Spain. I have already made arrangements there with an English merchant who has agreed to take you on as an apprentice clerk."

"A clerk?" John exclaimed. "I will not . . . !"

"You certainly will," his father replied with icy calm. "You have no choice."

"No!" John insisted. Jumping from his seat, he knocked into the dining table with such force that the candles tipped over, splattering melted wax everywhere. "I—"

"It is a most advantageous opportunity for you," his father said as he righted the candles. "A trade more suited to your personality, I think. You are dismissed."

✦

When Captain Newton set sail from Alicant, John was not aboard the ship. At the age of fifteen, he was alone in a foreign country among strangers, charged with learning a trade about which he knew nothing and cared less. If Captain Newton thought his son would rise to the occasion, he only demonstrated how little he knew John. Months later, when the Captain sailed back into Alicant harbor on his return trip, he found a most distraught merchant waiting at the dock to demand that he take John with him.

"He is smart all right," the merchant allowed, "but a more obstinate lad I never laid eyes on. I cannot teach him anything, because to his mind, he already knows more than I do. Take him, Sir, and be gone!"

The words seared Captain Newton through with humiliation.

He could not meet the eyes of his men as he loaded his son back on deck.

Since John had no assigned jobs, he searched his father's bookshelves for something to fill his days. What he found was a Bible, and he spent the majority of his time reading it and praying. And in the privacy of his father's cabin, or on some deserted spot on deck, he would lift his voice and sing a hymn as he used to with his mother:

> I sing the mighty power of God,
> That made the mountains rise;
> That spread the flowing seas abroad,
> and built the lofty skies. . . .

At meal time, he filled his plate with vegetables and bread, but when platters of braised meat and roasted chicken came his way, he shook his head and passed them along. "I'm fasting," he explained in answer to his father's raised eyebrows. Then he hurried back to his quarters for more meditation. And so it was day after day.

"Come upon the wind!" Captain Newton called brusquely to the helmsman.

"On the wind, Sir!"

"Unfurl the sails," Newton commanded. "I want every stitch of canvas drawing!"

"Unfurled and drawing, Sir."

With all sails out, they could proceed with utmost haste—should the winds continue to cooperate. The captain was most eager to finish gathering the cargo so he could batten down the hold and fix it with the company seals, then head for home. None too soon, in his opinion. He desperately wanted this voyage behind him.

With each passing day, Captain Newton's impatience grew. He couldn't pass by two sailors taking a bit of leisure without barking, "Back to work! A ship is no place for loafers!" Yet he was painfully aware that even as he chided others for their behavior, his own son barely spoke two words to anyone and never smiled. A man with the pox was more useful than he. The captain wasn't the only one to notice, either. Increased grumbling and bitter mockery proved as much.

Still, John was staying out of trouble. His father could give thanks for that. And for once, the cursing came from the mouths of others, not from his own son.

In time, John grew weary of his meatless diet. And as he laid his guilty conscience to rest, his old bad habits began to spring back. Not all at once, mind you. But a rude gesture here, a blast of cursing there, until finally what had seemed to be a newfound goodness was all but gone.

One day, as John and his father walked along a cobblestone lane in the Dutch port city of Middleburgh, John slowed his pace. "You go ahead," he called. "I want to look in this little bookshop." The second volume of *Characteristics*, written by Lord Shaftesbury, had caught his eye. Interesting title, he thought. Certainly worth a look. Once John picked it up, he couldn't put it down. Such wonderful words . . . speeches, romantic and fine . . . much wisdom and intelligence from his lordship!

John read, "What is right or wrong for one person doesn't necessarily apply to another."

*Fascinating!* he thought.

"It is up to each man to decide what is right for him."

*Now, this is real religion!*

John could hardly wait to get back to the ship to read the book. After he read it once, he read it again. Then again and again. He especially kept coming back to the second piece, entitled *Rhapsody*—so many times, in fact, that he could very nearly recite it in its entirety, word for word.

*All I have to do is follow this man,* John decided, *and finally I will find happiness.*

CHAPTER 4

# 1742

*"That book by Lord Shaftesbury, the celebrated free-thinker . . . operated like a slow poison and prepared the way for what was to follow."*

"LONG LIVE THE DYIN' 'ORSE!" A SAILOR CRIED OUT AS HE RAISED HIS tankard of bad liquor for yet another toast.

"The Dying Horse!" John Newton yelled, thrusting his tankard high. His father had ordered him back to the ship early, but what would he know? Surely the old man had fallen asleep hours ago! Or maybe he lurked somewhere in the Dying Horse Pub, spying on him. With lanterns so dim and the fog of tobacco smoke so thick, John couldn't even make out the mate in the next seat. Well, all the better.

It was sometime in the wee hours of the middle watch that John finally strutted back aboard the ship. When he approached his father's quarters, he paused as usual to take off his shoes. Tucking them under one arm, he turned the knob with a practiced hand, and silently pushed the door open just enough to admit his lean frame. Just as John was stretching out on his cot, a flame flared in the lantern overhead.

"So!" he father said. "You have returned at last."

"I'm seventeen years old!" John shot back. "I have a right to enjoy myself!"

"And also to pull your knife to the throat of an unarmed man?"

*He knows about the fight!* John thought. *How does he always know?*

"You are my son. When you were born, I gave you my name. I have my reputation to consider—"

"Your reputation!" John spat. "That's all you ever think about, isn't it? Well, I could tell you a thing or two about your precious reputation. . . ."

When was it John first became aware that everyone in town laughed at his father? Marching around pompously insisting he be called Captain. To his face, everyone was polite, of course. But when his back was turned, people would stand stiffly at attention, mock his march and salute, and say, "Yes, *Captain!*"

"I'll tell you what people say—" John began.

"No, I'll tell *you* what people say!" his father retorted. "That you, my son, are an irresponsible, unreliable, troublemaking idler with no ambition. *That's* what they say. And that reputation is not doing you any good!"

"I'm a ^&(!@# good sailor, and I—"

"Don't you use that language in my presence!" his father roared. "I am still your father—and your captain! And I'll tell you this much, John Newton, if I were not your father, I would have thrown you off my ship long ago!"

Fuming, John snatched up his belongings and tossed them into a pile. "I've been on your ship too long!"

"I completely agree," his father said. "Unfortunately, when I asked my friends to take you on, every one of them refused . Your reputation makes you a dangerous liability."

Perhaps it was the hopeless situation. Or maybe it was the toll of so many rigorous years at sea. But on his return to port, Captain

Newton announced his retirement. It was time for him to enjoy his wife and young sons. There was, of course, still the matter of John. An undisciplined sailor who would rather philosophize than work, with a reputation as a foul-mouthed troublemaker? Ah, no. No takers, regardless of his skill.

*How could a father and son be so different?* Newton mused. In his own years at sea, he had garnered a great deal of respect and friendship, not just from other officers, but from many in the shipping business. A fellow captain by the name of Joseph Manesty, for instance. After he left the sea, he became a successful merchant with an office in Liverpool. Expanded into shipbuilding, last Newton heard. Over the years, Manesty's holdings had grown impressive indeed.

✦

When his father summoned him, John dared not ignore, but he responded in a way that registered his disdain. Shuffling in an hour late, he assumed his most sullen posture. But his father simply ignored the tardiness and kept John waiting while he finished making notations in his notebook. Newton picked up the blotter and meticulously blotted the words one at a time, then carefully set his pen in its holder and replaced the top on the ink bottle. John sighed impatiently and shifted from one foot to the other. His father carefully closed the journal and centered it precisely on his desk. Only then did he look up at his son and motion for him to sit.

"You did not seem to want a life at sea, so I set you up with an apprenticeship in Spain," the elder Newton began. "But you, of course, knew better than your master. You argued with him and were so disagreeable he could not wait to get you out of his house."

Assuming his most practiced look of boredom, John sighed loudly. But a deep flush rose up to burn his face and betray his embarrassment. *That master had been a fool! Why couldn't my father see that? Why did he always have to blame me?*

"Your fortune is about to change—no thanks to you. Because of my connections, a whole new opportunity has been opened. And I would sorely admonish you to—"

"And just what is this great good fortune?" John asked sarcastically.

"My friend Joseph Manesty needs someone to oversee the slave operation on his sugar plantation in Jamaica, and I—"

Immediately John was on his feet. "Jamaica!? I don't—"

"It's already arranged. You'll get a good salary. And excellent prospects for the future. Manesty will be preparing you to take over the entire operation. Do a good job and you'll be back in five years with enough money to settle down to a comfortable life."

"But I don't—"

"You leave in two weeks. That gives you more than enough time to get yourself ready and still run an errand for me over in Kent."

"Now just you wait—"

"Two weeks, John. You are dismissed."

Captain Newton opened his journal and resumed writing. John jumped up and stepped toward his father. But thinking better of it, he stomped away fuming.

Five years! What right did his father have to make such a decision about his life? Still, as his indignation waned, John had to admit that it would be wonderful to be away from his father's constant eye. And when he came back, rich and independent, who would be respected then? Never again would anyone boss him around.

The next morning, John came into the kitchen just as his father was finishing his bowl of meal. William and Henry, John's young half-brothers, were still eating. Without a word of greeting, Tomasin got up from her place and served up a bowl for John along with a plate of fried fish. John pushed the fish aside and started in on the meal.

"Is John going to eat his fish?" William asked. "If he doesn't have to, I don't want to eat mine, either."

"Never you mind about John," Tomasin said through clenched teeth.

"I'll need you to ride to Maidstone for me today," Newton said. "You will be back in three days, four at the most. Plenty of time to prepare for Jamaica."

Though John had started to look forward to his new adventure, he wasn't about to give his father the satisfaction of knowing it. "Not one day of my life is my own, is it?" he snapped.

"And again I warn you . . . stay away from the docks," Newton continued, ignoring his son's rudeness. "Until you're officially on the ship, with your certificate of exemption in hand, you are fair game for the press gangs."

"Let them try!" John snorted. "My knife would serve me well."

"Just stay away from the docks." Then Newton added, "Oh, by the way . . . you have an invitation to pay a visit to the Catlett family while you are in the area."

"What?!"

"The Catletts. Old friends of your mother's, out in Chatham. No need to stay. Just stop and pay your respects, then be on your way. Won't take you an hour."

"You're shipping me off in three weeks! I don't want to spend my last days with some old worm-eaten. . . ." and John exploded into a storm of expletives.

Tomasin jumped to her feet. "That's enough!" she cried, slamming her spoon down on the table. "I will not have that kind of talk in my home!"

Turning his seething rage onto his stepmother, John yelled, "It just so happens, that *I* had a home before my father married you!"

William's mouth dropped open and he stared in dismay. Little Harry wailed. Before Tomasin could react, Captain Newton, his face livid, jumped to his feet.

"Go!" he bellowed at John. "Or don't go! I don't care! Just get out of my sight!"

John was on his feet and up the stairs. Within minutes, the front door slammed.

✦

Days later, shivering on horseback, John tugged at the woolen blanket he had thrown around him against the bitter cold. He prodded his horse to a gallop, past one snow-shrouded field after another. The uncommon December cold cut though the blanket and chilled his bones. How he longed for a comfortable chair beside a roaring fire. Oh, and a nice bowl of steaming hot soup would be lovely, too. His father's errand was done, and at this pace he could be home in two days. Two miserable, icy-cold days.

As John approached the narrow cobblestone streets of Chatham, he slowed his horse to a trot. The Catletts lived just a few miles off the road. Elizabeth . . . that was Mrs. Catlett's name. Same as his mother. Elizabeth Catlett, the one who came to care for her when she was so sick. The one who bundled her off in the carriage that day. . . .

Slowing the horse to a walk, John turned and headed down the street and onto a country lane. Well, it wouldn't hurt to say hello.

Maybe sit a minute by the fire. Perhaps have a bite to eat before heading for home.

John located the house—a good-sized two-story surrounded by a neatly painted white fence. It certainly looked inviting enough. He dismounted and tied his horse to a tree, then pushed the gate open. Suddenly a dog bounded toward him, barking furiously. In spite of himself, John cried out in alarm. Before he could recover himself, the front door opened.

"Excuse the dog, my lad," a jolly woman exclaimed, wiping her hands on her apron. "But he—"

She froze in mid-sentence. Gaping, the woman screamed, "Eeeeee, it's you!"

John jumped back, but Mrs. Catlett was too fast for him. She caught him and gripped him in a smothering embrace. "Lord, have mercy! You actually came!"

The door opened again and an entire flock of children poured out. As Mrs. Catlett pulled John toward the house, she called, "George! Come quick! Look who I found!" When Mr. Catlett made his way from the back of the house, Mrs. Catlett exclaimed, "It's just like his poor mother is back with us!" Then she dissolved into tears.

John, embarrassed and perplexed, looked from the sobbing woman to the gawking children then, imploringly, to George Catlett who stood stiffly by. After several moments of awkwardness, Mr. Catlett stepped forward, grabbed John's hand and shook it heartily.

"Welcome to our home, lad," he said. "You'll have to forgive my wife. Your mother was her dearest friend, and you do look uncommon like her."

Mrs. Catlett, composing herself, shooed the children into the house. Twelve-year-old Eliza took little Sara in while Jack, eleven, chased after Suzanna who toddled in the opposite direction. The oldest of the Catlett brood—fourteen-year-old Mary, whom they called Polly—had baby George in her arms.

"Here, now, you're shivering!" Mrs. Catlett said to John. "Come in and sit by the fire. We want to hear all about you."

After loading the best seat in the house with cushions and drawing it up close to the roaring fire, Mrs. Catlett presented it to John. Then Mary handed him a steaming bowl of lamb stew and bread hot from the oven.

"Ahhhhh," John sighed as he breathed in rich aroma of savory and rosemary.

Awkwardly, but with a sincerity that touched him deeply, Mrs. Catlett apologized for having left John behind when she took his mother away. "And you not yet seven years old," she said wiping her eyes. "But I was so certain I could nurse her well again. I was sure we would be back before summer ended. When that didn't happen . . . well . . . what I really wanted was to bring you here and raise you as one of our own. . . ."

*What a thought!*

"But I had to wait until your father returned. And then . . . then. . . ."

*Yes. Then there was Tomasin.*

"Well, under the circumstances, your father refused. And then we lost touch."

*How different life could have been!*

John sneaked a glace at Polly—should he be forward enough to call her that? Her family's pet name? Maybe not—and she gave him a shy smile. He found her to be a most agreeable young woman. Most agreeable indeed.

"Well!" Mr. Catlett said abruptly. "I say we've had enough

reminiscing for one night. Tell us about yourself, John. What have you been doing?"

John told about the sadness of his life that pushed him to sea. Then he regaled the family with tales of distant countries and fabulous adventures—some more true than others, but all featuring him as the hero. By the time he finally fell silent, the fire had burned low and the little girls were fast asleep.

"You do spin a good tale, Johnnie," Mrs. Catlett said with a sigh. "Did you know your mother planned on you being a preacher one day?"

Eliza and Jack laughed out loud. Even Mary couldn't suppress a giggle. Too many of John's stories were built around his mischief.

"Not much chance of that, Ma'am!" John said.

"Such a smart little boy," Mrs. Catlett said. "You made your mother so proud! Well, I'm sure whatever you do, you will do it well."

Her husband stood and stretched. "We have an extra bed, lad. You're welcome to stay with us as long as you wish."

When John first awakened to the muted beams of winter light, laughter echoing up the stairs and the fragrance of baking bread wafting in, he looked around him and blinked in confusion. He wasn't used to a soft bed and feather pillows. But then the whole wonderful evening came rushing back, and he bounded from bed and hurried into his clothes. Downstairs, to great cheers, Jack and Mr. Catlett were just coming through the back door laden with armloads of evergreen boughs.

"What's going on?" John asked.

"Christmas is coming!" four-year-old Sara cried, jumping up and down and clapping her hands. "Christmas is coming!"

"Your muscles, John. That's what we need!" Mr. Catlett exclaimed. "Jack and I are just ready to drag in the Yule logs, and they are plenty heavy!"

The entire family set to work decorating the house with boughs and candles and bows. "You'll stay and celebrate Christmas with us, won't you?" Mrs. Catlett asked.

"Well . . ." John said.

"Oh, do!" Mary encouraged. "We always have such fun!"

The following days were filled with excited merrymaking . . . and shut doors punctuated by whispers . . . and wonderful stories of Christmases past . . . and delicious fragrances from the kitchen. Every evening the entire family gathered to sing carols beside the fire and nibble on goodies because, Eliza laughed, "We can't wait until Christmas!" When John came down to the kitchen the morning before Christmas, Mrs. Catlett and Eliza were making plum pudding.

"Fresh Christmas goose!" Mr. Catlett called through the door as he and Jack stomped their shoes outside. They brought the goose in and Mary set to work plucking it.

Little Sara, her blue eyes dancing, grabbed John's hand and pulled him close. "Wanna know a secret?" she confided. "You're going to get—"

"Sara!" Eliza scolded. "Don't tell!"

John broke out in peals of laughter. He couldn't help himself. Sweeping the little girl up in his arms, he danced her across the kitchen floor. Never in his life had he enjoyed himself so thoroughly.

On Christmas morning, the family walked to church together through the snow. And when they got back home, there was a gift for everyone. John opened his to find a pair of hand-knit woolen socks. "I needed these this morning!" he laughed.

"That's your surprise!" Sara exclaimed, bouncing with glee.

Each morning John told himself, *Just one more day. Then I'll be on my way home.* But then he would look at Mary, and he would think about all that could happen in five years—she would be nineteen!—and somehow another day would pass by.

One morning as John and Jack split wood behind the house, John's wedge slipped and the heavy log rolled onto his foot. Before he could catch himself, a blast of curses poured from his mouth. Stunned, Jack dropped his ax and stared. "If Mother or Father heard that, you'd be out of here with a burning backside!" he said.

"Hah!" John snorted. "Little Johnnie, the boy who should be a preacher?" He picked up the wedge, jammed it back into the log, and went back to chopping wood.

Jack looked hard at the older boy. Even through his shirt, he could see the bulge of rock-hard muscles. So gentle he was, dancing with Sara in his arms. But now. . . .

"What are you really like?" Jack asked. "I mean, when you're not trying to impress my parents . . . or my sister?"

"No idea what you're talking about," John said without breaking his rhythm.

"Oh, come on. You've been here three weeks now, and I—"

John froze in mid-swing. "Three weeks? Has it really been that long?"

By noon, John was on his way back home, pushing his horse to a gallop whenever possible and otherwise riding at a full trot. He arrived exhausted and hungry, on a horse ready to drop. Before John's cloak was off, his father summoned him to his office.

"Once again I help you by asking a friend for a favor, and once again your irresponsibility lands me in a humiliating position!" Captain Newton roared. "What do you have to say for yourself?"

"That I had the best three weeks of my entire life," John answered. "That I finally know the meaning of a happy family. That I just met the girl I'm going to marry."

When Captain Newton finally managed to respond, he almost choked on the words, "Marry! The little Catlett girl? Are you completely out of your mind?"

"Why did I think I'd get any support from you?" John retorted. "I never have!"

John stormed out, slamming the office door behind him. And Captain Newton, who prided himself on running his life as tightly as he did his ship, slumped forward in his chair and sank his head into his hands.

For many hours, Newton remained in his office with the door closed. The more time went by, the more it worried John. Many were the times he had pushed his father hard, but he prided himself on knowing when to stop. Perhaps this time he had pushed too far. Deciding on the offensive approach, John practiced his most insolent look.

✦

Darkness had fallen by the time Newton finally stepped out of his office. John braced himself for the whipping of his life. Maybe he would even be thrown out of the house and ordered not to return. In a voice controlled and calm, Newton said, "Perhaps this was my fault. You might be right . . . it is time for you to make your own way."

John was thrown off guard. It wasn't like his father to give in so easily.

"At the end of the week you will leave on a merchant ship for Venice."

"Venice!" John exploded. "What happened to me making my own way?"

"That is precisely what you will do, my son," his father replied. "No more special privileges. No more taking refuge in the captain's cabin. You will be a common seaman where you can rise or fall on your own merits."

"You hired me out as a common seaman?" John exclaimed in disbelief.

"You seem to appreciate coarse jokes and profane oaths. I'm certain you will fit right in. You do have a problem obeying orders, but officers have a way of beating that out of seamen. Perhaps they can accomplish what I could not."

"I won't go!" John stated.

"Oh, yes you will," his father said in a voice that left no room for argument. "And to see that you do, I will be right at your side until the ship sails. After that, you are on your own. Completely. Just as you want to be."

CHAPTER 5

# 1743

*"I made a shipwreck of faith, hope, and conscience, and my love for Mary was my only remaining principle. The bare possibility of seeing her again was all that kept me from the most horrid designs against myself and others."*

JOHN SNORTED WITH DISGUST AS ONE-EYED CHARLEY WALKED PAST, slopping cooking oil onto the freshly scrubbed deck. "The likes of you should rot in prison!" John called after him. When Charley turned back, John cursed him soundly.

Maggot-ridden hard tack he could choke down (though he did sigh over memories of roasted lamb and baked bread at his father's table). And low wages he could abide (time would come when he would have his own ship). But work alongside these lowlifes? How much could he endure? Coarse and profane suited John just fine. He would gladly match wits and words with the foulest of them. But these fools could neither read nor write, and they didn't care to learn! Some, like Charley, had been let out of prison to sign aboard the ship. Others were so poor they sold themselves for the pittance the ship owner sent home to famished families.

"An' wot's it to ye where I come from?" Charley demanded.

"It's a lot to me," John sneered. "It's the likes of you that force the captain to use the whip on real sailors like me . . . for no offense at all"

"Yer mouth makes yer trouble, is wot!"

"Aw, to the devil with you!" John said as he turned back to his mop.

*My wonderful father! Dumps me on this rotten ship with good-for-nothing bums and criminals. He's probably sitting in his fine office right now laughing!* Such injustice! The more John thought about it, the more furious he grew.

Scrub decks and scrape railings. Sit with needle and thread mending coarse canvas sails until his fingers cracked and bled. Scour pots and more pots. Glancing up at the topmast, John spied a lad of no more than thirteen in the shrouds. That's where he longed to be—sitting on the yard, acting as lookout. He was good at it, too. Always had been. But no. He was stuck on the deck, doing the dirty work any fool could do. Suddenly he hated the young lad. If only he could make him lose his footing and fall headfirst to the deck. Or plunge into the churning sea. *Then I'd shimmy up that rigging and dance out on the yards for all to see!* John thought gleefully. He would show them!

Without his father's critical eye, John tossed the guard off his tongue. He made a point of listening carefully to the blasphemy older sailors spouted, and then—being the clever fellow he was—he picked it up and twisted it just so . . . and built on it just enough . . . until he could make even the toughest sailors blanch.

Old Mose, who had partaken of far too much rum for way too many years, stumbled against John's bucket of dirty water, slopping it onto the floor. John had just finished re-scrubbing after Charley's carelessness with the cooking oil.

"You sot of a fool! You drunken son of the devil!" John bellowed.

Confused, Mose jumped backwards—right into the bucket. Gray, oily water poured across the twice-scrubbed deck. Roaring in anger, John leaped at the befuddled sailor, grabbed him by the throat, and tossed him to the deck. Mose's head hit the planks with a thud. Growling curses, John straddled the hapless man and squeezed his throat. Mose, his eyes bugging, lifted his arms and flailed at John, but the feeble attempts came too late. Already his face had turned a dusky blue.

"You murderin' maniac!" bellowed a sailor who came to see what the commotion was all about. "You'd kill the poor fool fer takin' too much grog? It's you the devil's got!" He and Charley pulled John off. Just in time, too, for Mose was barely breathing.

John yanked loose from the men's grasp, then turned and kicked Mose in the ribs.

"'E's a mean one, 'e is," the older sailor said.

"Specially fer such a young bloke," Charley added, shaking his head.

For the most part, John's shipmates kept their distance, which was just fine with him. But when the ship dropped anchor in Venice, John joined the flood of sailors headed for shore. Much of the shouting and raucous laughing was punctuated with bawdy jokes and suggestive gestures as they all headed for the nearest tavern.

Dancing girls and flowing drinks . . . deafening noise and rowdy laughter. John was in his element. He plunked down a coin and grabbed a tankard of ale that would last him all evening. Still, he was every bit as loud and boisterous as his mates who put away many tankards. "I like to keep my wits about me," he laughed.

Eager to separate himself from the knot of sweaty men, John stepped away from the table. That's when he spied a particularly curvaceous girl with flowing black hair and smooth olive skin, which was well displayed by her revealing red satin dress.

"Well, now," John said, his appreciation bubbling. "And who might you be?"

"I might be Rose," she answered with a Spanish lilt and a teasing grin.

John reached out for her, but a drunken sailor stumbled into him and knocked him off his feet. Rose looked down at John sprawled on the floor, and she threw back her head and roared with laughter. Immediately, John sprang to his feet. Not the slightest trace of merriment shone on his face. Reaching down, he whipped a knife from his boot.

"Get away from me and this lady, you drunken sot, or I'll rip you up and light you like an oiled rag!" John hissed.

The sailor stared at him stupidly until Charley called out, "He'd do it, too!" Even in his drunken state, the sot had sense enough to stumble away. With a quick laugh, John slid the knife back into its sheath. Stepping up to the drunk, he clapped him on the back— and sent the man reeling. Then John turned back to the girl.

"But I'll do nothing of the kind when there's a Rose in the room," John said in a voice as sweet as pudding. He grabbed her and ran his hand up her back.

Rose laughed a coy giggle.

Without taking his eyes off Rose, John called back to his mates, "I'll see you back at the ship."

✦

At the sound of two bells in the middle watch, John staggered back on deck. Far after midnight. An hour certain to anger the captain.

John just shrugged and fell into his hammock. Soon he was fast asleep.

*Was it his watch? Was that why John was walking back and forth, back and forth, all alone? Wait . . . someone else was there. Someone with a ring for him.*

*"Keep it carefully," the person said solemnly. "As long as you have this ring, you will be happy and successful. But if you lose it . . . or if you willingly part with it . . . you will have nothing but trouble and misery."*

*Well, why not? Anyone could take care of a ring. But even as John was slipping it on his finger, another man came over and started asking questions.*

*"Special?" the man said. "Happiness and success, all because of that ring? Sounds silly. You're a man of reason. Throw it over the side and prove you don't believe in superstitions." What an absurd idea! John would do no such thing.*

*"So," the second man mocked, "you are not such a man of reason as you claim to be."*

*At that, John plucked the ring off his finger and dropped it over the side of the ship. Immediately, the mountains behind Venice burst into roaring flames.*

*"What have I done?" John cried, but it was too late.*

*"All the mercy God had for you was in that ring," the second man said, "and look how easily you tossed it away."*

*The ring! John had to go after it. Even though it meant throwing himself into the sea . . . maybe even through the flaming mountains . . . still he must go. Then the first man was back again.*

*"What's the matter?" he asked. When John admitted what he had done, the man shook his head and exclaimed, "What a fool you were!" Then he asked, "What if you had the ring back?" In that case, John promised, he would be wise and careful. Immediately the man jumped*

*over the side and into the water. When he reemerged, he had the ring.
At that moment the flames died in the mountains and the second
man—the seducer—disappeared.*

*"Thank you, thank you," John exclaimed joyfully as he reached out
for his ring. But the man pulled it away.*

*"Oh, no," he said. "If I gave it back, you would do the same thing
again. I'll keep it for you. When you need it . . . really need it . . . it
will be here for you."*

With a cry, John sat upright in his hammock. There was no
ring. It had all been a dream. But such a dream! So real. At first,
John could think of nothing else. He couldn't eat and he couldn't
drink. But as the days wore on, the dream began to fade, until in
time he forgot it completely.

✦

In the breathless air, sails hung limply from the mast. The sun beat
hard on the deck, and everyone who wasn't working fought for a
place in the scarce shade. John alone sat by the sun-baked rail staring out at the calm and glistening sea.

"What's eatin' at the likes o' you?" Charley called out as he
walked up from behind. "Ye ain't the kind to be seized with guilt."

John gave a start. When he saw who it was, he turned his back
and snapped, "Get your worthless hide out of here and leave me
alone."

"Who might she be?"

"Who?"

"The lass ye's dreamin' 'bout."

"Go away!" John repeated, his irritation rising.

Charlie planted himself on the deck, right next to John. "Ye think ye's the only lonesome one on this ship? I been away from me lady fer a whole year, too. Ain't even seen me littlest."

"It's been a whole year since I saw Mary," John moaned.

"Mary, eh? That yer sweet'art? Well, ye will see 'er by Christmas. Come Christmas, we be 'ome."

Christmas! Ah, just to recall the fragrance of the evergreen boughs and the sweetness of the plum pudding and the carols by the burning Yule log. Never again did John want to spend a Christmas anywhere but by Mary's side.

✦

When the ship sailed into London harbor, all British eyes were on the French fleet hovering off the coast. All except John Newton's. Something more important than war clouds was on his mind. He was going to see Mary. John barely thought about his own father, which is why Christmas in Essex didn't occur to him. Instead, he hired a horse and rode straight to the Catletts' house.

"It's me, John Newton!" he called out as he banged on the front door.

Once again warmly welcomed, John made himself at home. As night fell and the fire embers burned low, he showed no sign of slowing his boisterous narrative: ". . . and so I told him, 'Who do you think you are to boss me around?' I mean, those were the stupidest mates I ever did see. They had one old codger on that ship who was almost blind. Other misfits, too. And my dear father put me there with them!"

Mr. Catlett made no attempt to stifle a long yawn. "We can learn from all kinds of people," he said.

"You mean they could all learn from me!" John countered. "Including that fool of a captain."

"Were you smarter than him, too?" little Sara asked sleepily.

"You bet I was! One time—"

Abruptly, Mrs. Catlett got to her feet, scooped up Sara and carried her out. John didn't seem to notice. Without pausing for breath, he plunged right into another story. By the time he finally stopped talking, Suzanne had long since been tucked in bed, and Eliza and Jack were snoring in their chairs. Only Mary was still awake, and even she was fidgeting.

The next morning, Mr. Catlett, still yawning, made his way into the kitchen with an armload of wood to find his wife slamming breakfast bowls onto the table. He didn't have to ask the source of her irritation. John's bragging echoed through the closed door.

"How long will he stay?" Mrs. Catlett demanded.

"Through Christmas, he says," her husband answered with a resigned shrug.

Mrs. Catlett threw her large bread knife down on the cutting board. Then, hands on her hips, she confronted her husband. "Do you see the way he looks at Polly?"

Elizabeth Catlett was an extremely kind woman. Faithful and caring. Loving and generous to a fault. But she was also a woman who knew her mind. "Talk with him, George," she said. "I loved Elizabeth Newton like a sister, but you must do something."

That evening, while John—comfortably ensconced by the fire—was winding up another braggart tale, Mary abruptly stood and said, "I will bid you an early good night."

"Wait! I have something I want to say to everyone," John announced. "Mrs. Catlett, remember you once said that when I was little you and my mother talked about Mary and me growing up and marrying? Well, now that we're grown up, I want to ask for her hand in marriage."

Mary's face went pale. She stared at John as if he had lost his mind. Both her parents gaped, dumbfounded. Then Eliza started to laugh.

"Let's go out to the yard, John," Mr. Catlett said, struggling to control his voice.

John followed him, with Mrs. Catlett right behind. Mr. Catlett said, "Polly is much too young to consider marriage. Surely you can see that."

"Anyway, you aren't the type of person for her!" his wife exclaimed. "I mean, with your temperament. Maybe when she's older . . . if things change. . . ."

"And if you earn enough to support her properly," Mr. Catlett added.

Stunned and dejected, John hung his head. "I'll sign on a much more lucrative—"

"Don't count your eggs before they're in the pudding," Mrs. Catlett cautioned.

"I'll leave right after Christmas, and—"

"Mrs. Catlett and I think you should leave immediately."

"But, Christmas—" John begged.

"Go home, John," Mrs. Catlett said, not unkindly. "That's where you belong."

John made his way back to town, then he headed for the place he knew best . . . the dock. Shivering with cold, he slipped into the closest tavern. Although it was fairly full, the mood seemed somber. Suited John perfectly. He found a secluded corner where he could ignore the clinking glasses.

"Wot'll it be, mate?"

"Rum," John mumbled to the stout tavern keeper. He did not usually drink liquor, but this was not a usual night.

Suddenly, a tall man in the uniform of the British Royal Navy stood over him. John blinked in confusion at the cutlass in the sailor's hand. Before he could gather his wits, three others jumped him from behind. John managed to kick one in the face, but what chance did he have against four well armed men?

Even after they pinned him to the floor, John wouldn't give up. "Let me go, you *%##!" he swore. "Get your *&%# hands off me! You devils will rot in hell!"

The sailors pulled him to his feet, then half-pushed, half-dragged him kicking and screaming to the door. Every other patron focused his eyes on his own mug of ale.

"Bind him!" the officer in charge ordered.

John kicked the closest sailor in the face. Heaving his cudgel, the sailor landed a terrific blow to the side of John's head. Then the others grabbed him up by his arms and dragged him to a waiting row boat.

CHAPTER 6

# 1743

*"I think no case, except a conscience wounded by the wrath of God, could be more dreadful than mine. I was sorely tempted to throw myself into the sea and end my sorrows. . . ."*

"IN WITH YOU, YOU NO-GOOD TROUBLEMAKER!"

The sailors scooped John up and tossed him into the holding tank of a tender boat anchored in the bay. The overpowering stink of the place quickly jerked him to his senses. Gasping for breath in the stifling room, John struggled to pull away from the filthy men pressing in on him. It wasn't easy. The cell was packed with others as angry and befuddled as he. Muttering curses against the Catletts, John staggered to his feet. He swore at his father as he struggled to shove everyone out of his way. Lunging forward, he pounded and kicked at the bolted door, shouting curses at the sailors who captured him, at the British navy in general, at the King. Now and then he paused long enough to bellow, "Get my father, Captain John Newton! Bring him here . . . now!"

Four long, horrible days of seasick men, no toilets, and endless filth. Four days of choking down hardtack and stale water. Four days swinging between raging fury and floods of remorse for ignoring his father's warning to stay away from the docks. Four days of bellowed demands to summon his father.

"Heave her ho!" At the command, the tender boat started to move. When it finally stopped, the latch was unbolted and the men emerged to fresh air and their first sight of the *HMS Harwich*. Rope ladders, tossed down over the side, whipped wickedly in the wind.

"Up with you now!" an officer ordered. When the first man out shrank back in fear, the order was more stern: "Climb! Now!" In the end, it took the sharp point of a cutlass to force the terrified men up the ladders. All except John, that is. When the man in front of him quailed, John leapt forward, grabbed hold of the wildly swinging rope, and jumped on. He easily clambered to the top and on over the ship's railing.

Down in the tender boat, the officer smiled. "We did good with that one!" he said to his mates. "Should earn us an extra ration of rum."

The *HMS Harwich* was one of the newest vessels in the British Royal Navy's extensive fleet of warships, a full-rigged, 50-gun man-of-war. Weighing in at 976 tons, it required a crew of 350 to be fully manned. These additional fifty kidnapped men would certainly help. It was all perfectly legal, too. With England on the verge of war with France, the Royal Navy needed many hundreds more hands to crew the swelling fleet, especially experienced sailors. But few were willing to volunteer, however fine the warship. The life of a common sailor on a merchant ship might be bad, but compared to a seaman on a warship, it was paradise. Which is why sailors and officers of the Royal Navy were allowed—no, were *encouraged*—to snatch any able-bodied man they could, any way they could. Once on board a warship, he belonged to the Royal Navy.

The regimen of horror began immediately. Not only did the work never end, but every order was accompanied by a lash across the back. Even the slightest disobedience or failure to show respect resulted in more lashes. With John's seething anger and hatred of authority, his back was raw within days. No dining with officers at tables covered with linen and set with china and wine glasses, either. Oh, no. John squatted on the floor, pressed in with the other men, balanced a rough wooden trencher on his knee and ate with his fingers. No glowing candles, either. Just a couple of lanterns overhead, casting swaying shadows over the creaking bulkheads. And hardly did John sit down before it was back to work to the tune of the lash.

Driven to exhaustion, one man who came in with John cried out, "Better dead below than alive on board!" then he leapt over the side to his death. John was sorely tempted to follow him. But he still had one hope.

"If I could contact my father, Sir . . ." John began to Master's Mate Philips.

"The French are shooting at us," Philips answered. "Even if your father was in the House of Lords he couldn't get you off this ship."

Night was even more miserable than day. Hot and airless, the headroom below decks was so low it was impossible to walk upright. And with over two hundred hammocks slung just inches apart, the stale air, coupled with the overpowering stench of sweaty, unwashed men, was staggering.

After a month of exhausting days and smothering nights, all hands were summoned to the deck where Captain Carteret read out the Declaration of War.

"That's it," John moaned. "Now there's no way out."

Then, as John was sanding the railing in preparation for a fresh coat of finish, Philips approached him and announced, "Captain Carteret will see you in his office."

✦

Standing at attention in the captain's quarters, John's mind raced through his assorted acts of mischief and the men who could have turned him in. But the captain looked up from the paper in his hand and said, "John Newton, you are a lucky lad."

So. Someone heard his pleas after all. Someone did notify his father. In fact, his father had traveled to see the officers of the Royal Navy to personally appeal for his son's release. Unfortunately, it could not be done. Not in war time.

"I know your father and the great job he's doing for the Royal Africa Company," Captain Carteret continued. "And I must say, I admire him greatly. So I'm going to honor his personal request to me and promote you to midshipman."

"Yes, Sir!" John said. "Thank you, Sir."

"Mr. Newton," the captain continued. "However hard you may think your life is here, you may thank God and your father that you are no longer a mere seaman. Make yourself worthy of this appointment."

"Yes, Sir! I will, Sir," John said as he executed a smart salute.

It was the responsibility of Lieutenant James Mitchell to move John from below decks up to the quarter deck, and he took the job seriously.

"You're the officer now, they're the below decks," Mitchell said, nodding toward John's former mates. "You call orders and they jump to. Forget any friendships you might have made. Unless you show strength, they will end up despising you."

"Yes, Sir," John said.

"Earn their respect. That's your greatest job," Mitchell added.

As the two officers walked fore, they passed three seamen working on the railing.

"Fanning!" Lieutenant Mitchell ordered. "To the top of the mast with you!"

Fanning hesitated. Only when Mitchell reached for his whip did the seaman move toward the rigging. At the last minute, though, he froze.

"Hah! Some sailor you are!" Mitchell called. "Get you to the lubbers hole then!"

With a sigh of relief, Fanning scurried through the hatchway and up into the rigging via a safer route.

"How about you?" Mitchell said to John. "Would you go aloft in the rigging and the shrouds?"

"Any day or night, Sir," John responded. "Just give the word."

Once again, John sat at a linen-covered table and filled his china plate with decent food. "Hear, Hear!" he called, raising his glass in a toast to Captain Carteret. When night came, he lay in a bunk with a pillow at his head. Ahhh, the life of an officer!

No need to warn John against making friends with the men. Not with the way he strutted before his former mates and treated them with haughty contempt. But neither did he earn their respect. His sarcastic remarks and jokes about their stupidity saw to that.

"Fanning!" John called as he worked with a group of seaman on the sails. "Learn to climb the rigging yet? Or do you still crawl in the back door like a fat old woman?"

Scowling, Fanning ignored him. But when John accused him of insolence and brought a lash down across his back, Seaman Bank stepped up, fists clenched and ready to fight. Laughing, John assumed a mocking fight-stance of his own. But before John could push them further, a burst of commotion echoed from the far side of the ship. Forgetting all about Fanning, John ran over to see what was happening. One seaman was on another's back, yanking his head backward by a fistful of hair. Both men bellowed, but the real noise came from the men gathered around, choosing up sides and laying bets.

A young officer marched up and ordered, "Break it up!"

The fighting continued. So did the betting.

With a snap of his whip, John sent both men sprawling.

"Any more fighting and you'll both be clapped in irons!" John threatened. "The rest of you . . . back to work!" Another lash for emphasis, and everyone scattered.

"Thank you," the young man said with obvious relief. "I'm still learning to show my strength. Name's Job Lewis—Midshipman."

"John Newton—same. What happened here?"

"That troublemaker, Mick Bass, again," Lewis said. "He's nothing but bad."

Same could have been said of John Newton. He seemed to take special pleasure in humiliating the seamen. Before long, only two men still liked him: Lieutenant Mitchell and Midshipman Lewis. A fact that did not bother John Newton in the least.

As an officer, John was no longer confined to the ship. As soon as the captain gave him a twenty-four hour liberty, he boarded a longboat with the other officers and headed for shore. But he didn't come back with the others. Instead, he rode out to see Mary at her boarding school. Strutting about in his bright blue uniform, he boasted that he would soon be captain of his own vessel. Mary's friends laughed and mocked him and made faces, but it didn't seem to bother John at all. Mary, however, was humiliated.

"Go back to your ship," Mary said. "And don't come back to see me again."

"But can I still visit you at your home on holidays?" John asked.

Mary shrugged. But she didn't say no.

So, already making plans for the next time, John went back to the ship several days late. Captain Carteret was waiting for him.

# CHAPTER 7

# 1744

*"My rash actions highly displeased the captain and lost me favor which I never recovered."*

"ALL HANDS PREPARE FOR BATTLE! ALL HANDS PREPARE FOR BATTLE!" Drummers joined the call to arms, their cadence echoing off the bulkheads and flooding the decks.

Assigned to protect convoys in the English Channel, the *Harwich* had traveled up to Scotland, then across the North Sea to Belgium, Sweden, and Denmark. Now she was back off the English coast where the danger from French ships was greatest.

In the munitions hold, lids flew off crates as men grabbed arms from stacks of swords, pistols, and muskets fixed with bayonets. As the gun crew rolled out barrels of gunpowder, each gun's captain and loader prepared round shot for the 18-pounders.

"All hands to your stations! All hands to your stations!"

Still buckling on their swords, the men ran up the stairs to the top deck.

Captain Carteret lowered his spyglass and announced, "French. Full sails, lads!"

John Newton squinted in the direction the captain indicated. All he could see was an expanse of choppy sea. Then, just a speck at first, then larger and larger until . . . yes, a full-rigged warship. It was the French frigate *Solide*.

As the distance between the ships narrowed, Captain Cartaret called, "Open fire!"

The first shots fell short, splashing into the sea. Not the volley of broadside shots that followed, however. As it smashed the *Solide* starboard, the *Harwich* crew broke into wild cheers.

"'Tis over, Mates! The prize is ours!" Fanning cried as he broke into a wild jig.

But the *Solide* wasn't about to quit. Damaged though she was, she resumed firing.

"We must all pray, Sir," suggested a nervous Job Lewis.

"Aye," Captain Cartaret answered. "So long as we reinforce our prayers with gunpowder and steel."

As the *Solide* began a slow advance, Captain Cartaret ordered, "Spill the wind from the sails and bring us to a stop." Then, "Come about and prepare to fire! Two broadsides from us for every one of hers!"

But even as the orders were called, the *Solide* slowed. Then she struck colors, lowering her flag in a sign of surrender.

"Ahhh, my lads," the captain said with a smile. "*Now* it is over!"

This time such a round of cheers erupted that it rocked the deck.

"Boarding party, Mr. Philips!" Captain Cartaret ordered. "Take the survivors as prisoners of war and bring the captain to me."

"Come on, James," Philips called to Mitchell. "You too, Newton."

As renewed cheers roared from the *Harwich* crew, the Master's Mate led the hastily gathered boarding party over to the *Solide*. To even greater cheers, they returned with the French captain in tow. Never mind that he was so seriously injured he had to be carried.

When he handed his sword to Captain Carteret, the surrender was official.

"Inspect the damage, Mr. Wainwright," Captain Carteret told the ship's carpenter. "Mr. Lewis, count our casualties. Add up the casualties among the French, Mr. Newton."

✦

Sails and rigging on the *Harwich* sustained damage, but everything else seemed fine. Wainwright gathered a crew and immediately set about making repairs. Only one *Harwich* crewman was lost. The *Solide*, however, limped badly. Seven Frenchmen lay dead and twenty others seriously injured, including the French captain who lost his leg.

"You did a good job today," Captain Cartaret told his men. "An extra ration of grog for all. The captured ship will be sold and the profits divided among us according to rank. I can assure you, everyone will get something."

At this, the crew went wild.

Spoils of war! John hadn't even considered that. And as a midshipman instead of a seaman. . . . His eyes glowed at the possibilities.

How John longed to sink into his bunk early, douse the light, and let the gentle rocking of the ship carry him off to a long, deep slumber. Every muscle of his body ached and his head throbbed. But he was officer of the watch. And so, while his mates snored below, John paced the deck, cursing under his breath at his rotten luck.

Ambling to the bow, John leaned out over the railing and surveyed the sky. The crescent moon floated free of the clouds. Quickly he traced the constellations, racing to see how many he could locate before the clouds swallowed them up. Even after the stars and moon had all but disappeared, John stood at the railing listening to the music of water sloshing against the ship's hull. He had no way of knowing that just below him a shadow moved through the sailors' berth, silently inching its way between the swaying hammocks. . . . that it paused beside one and clamped a hand over the mouth of the seaman sleeping there. He could not see the horror in the seaman's eyes just before his throat was sliced with a knife that should have been replaced in the munitions hold.

Before the sun was up, all hands were summoned to the deck. John Newton stood at attention between Job Lewis and James Mitchell.

"All present and accounted for, Sir," Masters Mate Philips reported.

"Then the killer is among us," said Captain Carteret.

After a few words, the dead seaman's body, already sewn up into his hammock, was slid into the sea. Then the captain tersely announced, "All crew is on half rations until I know the identity of the killer."

A curse mumbled from out of the ranks was cut short by Philip's whip.

"And no grog for anyone!" the captain growled. "Any more comments?"

Silence.

"I will be in my cabin until first bell in the afternoon. Messages concerning the identity of the murderer can be sent to me. If he is not apprehended by this time tomorrow, rations will be halved again. You are dismissed."

It didn't take long. At three bells forenoon, Job rushed up to John with the news. "It was Mick Bass. Turned in within the hour. Killed the bloke he was fighting on deck."

"Why did he have to *kill* the poor devil?" John asked.

Job shook his head. But Mitchell called over, "Because he's Mick Bass, that's why. A murdering son of a demon scraped out of prison and slopped onto our deck."

"Hey, give some gratitude!" another junior officer by the name of Brant chimed in. "Given the choice between prison and our fair ship, he chose us!"

By now, half a dozen young officers had joined the gathering. "What's the difference?" said one. "A man-o-war is nothing but a prison anyway."

"Worse," Brant said. "Here, if the rats don't get you, the rising seas will."

"I'm betting Captain will teach Mick a lesson he won't forget," John ventured.

Everyone roared with laughter. Everyone except Job, who seemed genuinely troubled by the entire business.

Late in the afternoon, the crew was again summoned on deck. Mick Bass, stripped almost bare, was bound hand and foot to an iron grid. Bellowing oaths and threats, he struggled against his bonds.

"On His Majesty's warship *Harwich*, I will not tolerate undisciplined behavior," Captain Carteret announced in a steely cold voice. "For the crime of murder I hereby sentence Mick Bass to twenty-five lashes with the cat-o'-nine-tails." Then to Mick he said, "May God have mercy on your soul."

With a gasp, Mick's belligerence vanished. "No, cap'n!" he whined. "Not twenty-five !"

The boatswain's mate stepped forward. At the captain's command, he brought the cat down hard across Mick's bare back— once, then twice. By the third lash, Mick was screaming. By the fifth, he begged for mercy. Still, the lashing continued. The flying cat sent blood spraying across the deck as Mick's screams melted into anguished moans.

With Job sobbing quietly beside him, John squeezed his eyes closed. Still he could hear the horror of slashing flesh and tortured groans. At last, when all was silent, John opened his eyes to see Mick hanging limp and the deck running red with his blood.

"He is dead, Sir," the boatswain's mate stated matter-of-factly.

Without the least show of emotion, Captain Cartaret pronounced, "Let this be a lesson to all of you. I *will have* discipline aboard this ship." Then he said, "You are dismissed."

Within minutes, John Newton stood alone on the bloody deck. He could not wrest his eyes from the man whose back had been reduced to shreds.

✦

That evening, on his way to dine, John was surprised to see that the deck timbers had already been sanded smooth and washed clean. By tomorrow they would have a new coat of finish. Just as if Mick had never been born. Surprisingly, the other officers didn't seem particularly concerned about what they had witnessed.

"I, personally, don't see how anyone with intelligence can try to answer the questions of the universe with anything except reason," Lieutenant Mitchell insisted between mouthfuls of roast chicken. When neither John nor Job responded, he continued, "Now, Captain Cartaret is certainly an intelligent man. So, why would he say to a worthless bugger like Mick Bass, 'May God have mercy on your soul'?"

"He didn't mean anything by it, James," John said irritably. "It was just something to say."

"If anyone needed mercy, it was Mick," Job pointed out.

"Hah!" Mitchell sneered. "If there was a God—which I firmly deny—he would certainly have better things to do than fool with the likes of old Mick."

"God's ways are not our ways," Job quoted from scripture.

"God's ways aren't any ways, because God is nothing but a myth for children and fools," Mitchell retorted. "It's about time you grow up, laddie, and move beyond such superstitions. Right, John?"

For a minute John said nothing. Then he asked, "Ever hear of Lord Shaftsbury?"

"Sure," Mitchell said. "Great philosopher. Now there's someone with intelligence."

"I got a copy of his book *Characteristics* and I must say, it is interesting reading."

"Yeah? I'm always looking for a good book," said Job. "What does he say?"

"That life is a lot simpler and more fun if you throw out the outdated idea of sin."

"If you don't have sin, you don't need to believe in God," Mitchell added. "And if there's no God, there's no heaven and no hell. Ergo, a thinking man has the right to believe however he sees fit."

"All you have to do is look around and you will see the proof of sin," Job challenged. "Now, Mick's punishment . . . it just might be punishment from God."

"Stop right there," Mitchell demanded, pointing a chicken bone in Job's face. "So you're suggesting we should do the right thing for fear of God's punishment? That's not righteousness—it's selfishness!"

"And immortality?" John sneered. "Nothing but bait to lure

people to church. Yet so many fools meekly follow like a bunch of stupid sheep!"

Job opened his mouth to argue, but he thought better of it. Desperately he looked around the table for someone to take his side. But everyone else was engaged in a conversation of his own. No one wanted to talk philosophy . . . or religion.

"So the only rational course is to live however we see fit," Mitchell was saying. "And how I see fit is to get the most I can out of life. After all, who knows when we might end up overboard? Or roasting with fever?"

"Or like old Mick, stripped of our skin?" said John.

From that day forward, John searched out opportunities to mock Job's religious beliefs and scorn his moral lifestyle. Job did his best to obey the rules, but John was always right behind him with a ridiculing jab and a blasphemous joke. Then he added, "It's for your own good."

Job, not easily daunted, struggled earnestly to defend his Christian faith. "The miracles of Jesus—" he would begin, only to be cut off with derisive comments about the stupidity of anyone who would fall for such superstitious foolishness. He did his best to match wits with John, but every discussion ended up in a hot argument.

✦

Days passed, and the ship continued to lie at anchor just off shore. With little to occupy his time, John grew increasingly restless. Even philosophical sparrings began to bore and irritate him. Just when he thought he could take no more, Lieutenant Mitchell announced, "John! I got shore leave for you and me and Job!"

With John in the lead, the three swaggered to the dockside marketplace.

"So, mates," said Mitchell, "shall we pleasure the ladies with our company?"

"Keep them waiting, and they'll appreciate us all the more," John answered. "I have my mouth set for something worth eating." It didn't take a sailor long to begin coveting fresh food. Even at the officers' table, with its greatly improved menu, fresh fruit and vegetables quickly became a rare luxury. John picked an apple from a green grocers booth. "How much?" he asked.

"Ha' penny," the grocer said.

"Ha' penny!" John exclaimed. "For one apple? That's thievery!"

"Pay me price or leave it be," the grocer said with a shrug.

With exaggerated disdain, John tossed the apple back, cursing loudly. The grocer, deciding the cheeky lad wasn't worth any more of his time, turned back to his work. Like a flash, John whipped up an armload of apples and was off running.

"Here, now! Don't ye be stealin' me wares!" the grocer hollered as he gave chase. "I'll have the law after ye, I will!"

But the grocer was fat and slow, and John was young and fast. Soon the grocer was alone in the road, panting and shaking his fist. When Mitchell and Job caught up with John, he was sitting under a tree biting into a stolen apple and laughing heartily.

"My belief is that I should have my fill of fresh apples without having to pay a ludicrous price," he announced. "Even better, without having to pay any price at all!"

Lieutenant Mitchell shook his head. "My belief is that I don't want to lose my commission for stolen apples!"

"You two want to turn out dull and boring like old man Cart

o' Rats?" John sneered as he tossed them each an apple. "He may scare you, but he doesn't scare me!"

Jumping up, John called out, "Hey, Job, watch this!" He crept over to a shop with several horses tied up in front. Quickly he untied them and with a yell slapped them on the flanks. As one, they took off at full gallop. The owners ran out of the shop to see what was going on, then took chase, yelling and cursing. John laughed so hard he couldn't stand up. Although Mitchell also laughed, he was careful to stay a safe distance back. As for Job—he smiled, but only with the greatest unease.

When the excitement died down, Mitchell said, "My further belief, Sirs, is that we should not keep the ladies waiting any longer. We must be back aboard ship before midnight watch."

John, on his feet and ready to go, laughed his agreement. Job Lewis, however, turned around and silently made his way to the ship.

At some point, Lieutenant Mitchell also returned to the ship, but John was in no hurry. The first bell of morning watch had already sounded before he got back. At first light, Captain Cartaret summoned him.

"I am extremely displeased," the captain said. "Over four hours late! Furthermore, I received disturbing news about your behavior. What do you have to say for yourself?"

"I offer my apologies, Sir. I'm afraid I had too much to drink."

"That is not an excuse befitting an officer of the Royal Navy."

"Yes, Sir. It will not happen again, Sir."

"You see that it doesn't!" the captain barked. "I am not known for giving second chances. But for your father's sake, I'll make an exception. You are dismissed."

"Yes, Sir. And thank you," John said as he executed a smart salute.

But once outside, John made an ugly face and threw a crude gesture toward the captain's office. "You be %!@$&, you son of a bleeding devil," John spat. "I'll see you in hell before I grovel on the deck before you."

✦

With little to do aboard ship, Lieutenant Mitchell and John had plenty of time to discuss Lord Shaftsbury's ideas. Even though John belittled Job for his religious views, and despite John's readiness to spout blasphemy, Mitchell chided him for trying to tie New Testament Christianity in with Shaftsbury's free-thinking ideas.

"Reason?" Mitchell challenged. "Rational thinking? Not until you get beyond that religion." Shaking his head, he added, "It's too bad. I would expect it from Job. But you . . . I thought you were too smart for all that foolishness. Guess I over estimated you."

As December approached, John's thoughts turned to Christmas. A merry time at the Catletts' house . . . wonderful days and cozy evenings with Mary. . . .

"Dreaming about your girl?" Lieutenant Mitchell had come up behind and interrupted John's reverie. John didn't answer. He continued staring out to sea.

"Hope you said a sweet goodbye," Mitchell said. "We're going to accompany a convoy of Royal African Company ships to Gambia, then to India. We'll be out five years."

"Five years?!" John exclaimed. "I've got to get leave from Captain Rat!"

"Oh, he'll be real happy to oblige you! Especially since he's canceled all leaves."

John snorted. "I can still handle the likes of him."

CHAPTER 8

# December 1744

*"It was a maxim with me in those unhappy days never to deliberate."*

"I BEG YOU, SIR!" JOHN IMPLORED. "I MUST SAY GOODBYE TO MY . . . my Mary."

"And just why should I extend any favors to you?" Captain Cartaret demanded. "I canceled all shore leave, even for dependable, pleasant crewmen. Why, pray tell, should I make an exception for a troublemaker who makes my life miserable?"

"For my father's sake," John pleaded. "Please. Give me one more chance."

Though the captain's glare never wavered, his heart did. He could, after all, remember being young and in love. And there was Captain Newton to consider.

"Twenty-four hours, then," he sighed. "Against my better judgment, mind you!"

"Oh, thank you, Sir! Thank you!" John cried.

"But you had better not be late!" he warned. "Not one minute!"

John ran to the closest livery where he hired a horse, then he took off for Chatham at a full gallop. If all went well, and if he spent no more than ten minutes with Mary, he would be back on time.

Almost before the weary horse came to a stop, John leapt off and ran toward the house. At the very same moment Mary came around from the side.

"Why are you here?" Mary demanded.

"My ship is sailing for the East Indies and I'll be gone for five years," John said. "*Five years,* Mary! I couldn't go without—"

Before he could finish, Mr. Catlett opened the door. "John!" he exclaimed. Mrs. Catlett came running too, and all the children followed. It wasn't the joyous reception John had received before, but since everyone assumed he had come to spend Christmas, and because they were hospitable people, they invited him to sit by the fire and enjoy a bowl of stew. John gazed at the house where he had known such warmth and happiness, and where the aroma of fresh baked bread was escaping deliciously from the kitchen. *Just a few minutes by the fire,* he thought. *Just a few bites before my long ride back. . . .*

In the end, he stayed the night. Then the next day, and the next night. And after that . . . well, what did it matter then? All John could think of was the merriment of Christmas with Mary and her family. He sat in church with a clenched jaw, and he sang carols about the birth of God's Son with a fake smile. An atheist pretending to believe.

"Five years I'll be gone," John told Mary. "But it will go fast. And you will still be young when I return. Promise you'll wait for me?"

Not the least bit interested in making such a promise, the most Mary would agree to was writing him a letter. Perhaps. Possibly two.

After six days in Chatham, John was bragging as usual about his sharp wits when he accidentally let it slip that his captain had granted him only one day's leave.

"What?" Mr. Catlett exploded. "You mean you are a deserter?"

"Of course not!" John laughed. "I just overstayed my leave a bit."

"A bit!" Mr. Catlett exclaimed. "We are a country at war! How could you be so irresponsible? I want you out of my house. As for my daughter, I forbid you to see her again!"

"But, Sir. . . ."

"Leave! Now! And don't attempt to contact my Polly."

✦

Mr. Catlett, as it turned out, was only the beginning of John's troubles. He returned to the ship to find the captain livid. "No one else gets shore leave," he roared. "Only you, because I took pity on you. One day, I said. One single day! Now, here you come dragging back a week late! Never will I trust you again, John Newton!"

Captain furious. . . . Catletts' door slammed shut. . . . Mary denied to him. And five endless years away. John sat on the deck, staring morosely across the water at London. Dark despair enshrouded him. Anchor not yet lifted, no sail hoisted, yet he may as well have been locked away on a prison island.

"When it comes to someone claiming to believe in a supreme being, I think—"

"Shut your lip, James!" John growled. He wouldn't even turn around to face his friend. "Who cares what you &*%! believe? You're no—"

"Hey!" Mitchell shot back. "It's not my fault you made the captain so angry."

"Five years at sea. Mary won't wait for me. She will be lost to me forever."

"Nothing you can do about it," Mitchell said with a shrug.

Although John watched ship after ship sail past, he had no idea of the enormity of the fleet assembling off England's coast. A total of 116 warships, flanked by merchant and store ships, were preparing to leave from Portsmouth Sound. And the well-armed *Harwich* was charged with protecting them. Her long guns could sink shot three feet deep in solid oak at a range of 400 yards. Even at 1,000 yards, they could penetrate more than a foot.

On a blustery February morning, the *Harwich* finally set sail, passing through the Strait of Dover and on into the English Channel. At last, they were underway. But not for long. In Spithead, just off the Isle of Wight, they dropped anchor, and there the entire fleet sat for another three weeks awaiting more ships.

*What I could be doing in England!* John steamed.

Finally, with the full squadron at last assembled, it was a magnificent sight to behold—billowing sails, pennants flying, ships sailing in perfect formation. But just three days out, the wind turned, forcing the fleet to take refuge in Torbay. Not until the last day of February did fair weather finally return and allow them to begin again. Then on the coast of Cornwall, just as the fleet rounded Lizard Point, a violent storm hit.

Ships blown off course sailed directly in front of one another, turning the tight sailing formation into a death trap. Some who tried to escape crashed on the treacherous rocks. All through the confusing day and throughout the moonless night, sailors fought desperately to control their ships.

"Unfurl the sail!" Captain Cartaret ordered. "Lower the jib!"

Several times the *Harwich* came within a few feet of neighboring vessels, but Captain Cartaret, a superb seaman, was able to avoid disaster.

"Quick is the word and sharp is the action!" he called to the men.

Although many things demanded the captain's attention, he could not help noticing John dashing surefooted up the rigging without so much as a slip or a stumble. Such ability . . . so much potential. "Pity," he sighed, shaking his head.

When the sun came up next morning, the fleet's massive damage was obvious. Several vessels lost . . . the flagship missing her mainsail. The entire fleet limped into Plymouth for repairs. "Should take about a month," carpenter Wainwright reckoned.

Captive on the ship for the entire month of March? Before, it was only John who hung about the deck, morose and depressed. Now, the entire crew wallowed in despair. It didn't help that they could stand on deck and gaze over at Plymouth . . . at life and freedom. For a good swimmer, just a short swim away. And so, every night in the dark of the moon, seamen—and some officers, too—slipped over the side of the ship and simply disappeared.

John's father, who had secured a position with the African Company, owned an interest in some of the damaged ships. When John heard that his father would oversee the damage report, he thought, *If he's in such close communication with the high-ranking officers of the fleet, he might be able to get me transferred into the African service.* Suddenly, working under Captain Newton didn't seem half so bad. But John could never get a letter to him in time. His only hope was to see him in person.

"Please, please, Sir!" John begged the captain. "My father is right on shore. All I need is a couple of hours and I'll be right back."

Captain Cartaret fixed John in a disdainful glare. "I cannot believe you even have the nerve to come here and ask me such a favor!" he said.

"Oh, I wouldn't, Sir," John replied. "But I'm not doing anything on the ship anyway. And if I could just talk to my father—"

"Do you take me for a fool?" the captain demanded.

"Oh, no, Sir! I—"

"You are the most irresponsible, dishonest, unreliable trouble-maker I ever had the misfortune to encounter in all my years at sea!" Captain Cartaret proclaimed. "And I assure you, that takes some doing. No way would I ever trust you."

"But Sir, if only—"

"Leave my quarters! And do not mention this again."

On his way out, John stopped to gaze over the side of the ship where so many had slipped to freedom . . . or death. He would gladly do the same, if he could swim. Not that drowning seemed such a bad option. Still, the thought of those cold waves closing in over his head. . . .

✦

In early April, after John had endured more than he ever thought possible, Lieutenant Mitchell approached him with an assignment. "Captain's sending the longboat to shore to collect fresh water and biscuits and round up deserters. Want to go?"

"Why me?" John responded morosely. "Why not Job or Brant? Or you?"

"Has to be someone who can't swim a stroke," Mitchell responded. "Captain's orders. You immediately came to mind."

At the order, each man chosen climbed down the ladder and took his place on the longboat rowing bench. Since John was the only officer in the party, he was in charge. When the men pulled the boat up on shore, John assigned three to go for water and three more to get the biscuits. Then to Hank, the older sailor still beside him, he said, "We'll go into Plymouth and search for deserters."

"Not into town," Hank said. "Cap'n's orders."

"Where else would deserters be?" John demanded. "Anyway, my father's there and he could help—"

"We obey cap'n's orders!"

"All right," John said. "Let's split up and—"

"No!" Hank insisted. "We sticks together. Them's—"

"—captain's orders," John said. "Yeah, I know!"

Life at sea was exceedingly hard, especially for men such as Hank, the lowest of the seamen. Few lived to see their thirties. John had no idea of Hank's age, but with his leathered skin and toothless gums, he seemed ancient. What could persuade such a man to remain so steadfast to the captain's orders? Didn't he ever give a thought to what might best for *him?*

Actually, John didn't dislike old Hank. But John had to think of John. So he crossed behind the old seaman as if to grab the mooring warp, but instead he picked up a rock and cracked Hank over the head. "Sorry, Mate," he said, "but I've got to get out of here." Then he disappeared into the crowded quayside.

John ran fast enough to put as much distance as possible between himself and the longboat, but not fast enough to attract undue attention. Once he reached his father, he would be fine, but until then, he must not rest. He raised his coat collar against the cold, raw wind. Really, he should take the coat off and hide it under a tree. The Royal Navy uniform would surely rouse attention. But the cold. . . .

After the first day and a half, John grew weary. Sleep was out of the question. Even at his brisk pace, he still had well over a day's walk ahead of him. But as he grew close to Torbay—and to his father—new energy washed over him. Only a few miles left, and no one had given him so much as a second look! Whistling, John marched up a low hill and started down the other side, enjoying the first signs of spring. But what he saw below froze him in his tracks. A small party of men in bright red jackets . . . marines!

Frantically, John searched for a place to hide—a woods or a thicket. But all around was nothing but open field. And then the marines spotted him. Before John could think, they galloped forward and surrounded him.

"I'm on leave!" John shouted in desperation.

"Your documents, then," demanded one.

Assuming a defiant stance, John declared, "I don't have to obey orders from you! I say I'm an officer on leave, and I am a man of my word!"

"We think you're the deserter from the *Harwich*," the marine replied as he raised his musket to John's head. "Let's see what the captain thinks."

So violently did John kick and fight that the marines couldn't get the ties on his wrists. "You're going back!" the first marine yelled. "Will it be with your wrists bound or a bullet in your head?"

It was no use. Arms bound and legs in chains, John was marched the twenty-four miles back to Plymouth. Once in town, the marines paraded him down the main street at gunpoint. Men ceased their talk to stare. Women stopped haggling with vendors to gape.

"Deserter!" shouted a young lad.

"Dirty pig!" yelled a woman who had a little child clinging to her skirts.

As others joined in and showered John with insults, a man strode up and spit in his face. "It's wot ye deserves, traitor!" the man growled.

A vegetable vendor grabbed a rotten tomato off the ground and hurled it. His aim was perfect. The tomato splatted against the side of John's head.

With each humiliation, John's heart burned with shame and indignation.

"In wi' ye, now!" the marine ordered as he shoved John into the Plymouth guardhouse and clamped him in irons. "Bread and water ye gits. If ye wants more, beg it from yer captain on the *Harwich*."

For two entire days John shivered . . . and ached . . . and starved . . . in the guardhouse. But most of all, he thought. And his thoughts set him to trembling. The penalty for desertion in time of war was hanging by the neck from the yardarm until dead. Or, if the captain took kindly to him—extremely doubtful—one hundred lashes with the cat-o'-nine-tails. Visions of Mick Bass flashed before his eyes: The lash flaying Mick's back. . . . Mick screaming for mercy. . . . Mick's body lying on the bloody deck.

Finally John was rowed out to the *Harwich* where Captain Cartaret awaited him. "Clamp him in irons," the captain ordered in a voice as cold and hard as icy steel.

As soon as John's father heard what had happened, he rushed to the ship to plead for his son. "Exchange him to a merchant ship," he implored. "Please. My son has much maturing to do, but he is a good sailor. You know that."

But Captain Cartaret was not in a bargaining mood. "I have many young men in my service who possess much less skill and prowess, and who are less intelligent than John. Yet I would be far more inclined to entrust my ship—indeed, even my own life—to them," he replied. "Talent and ability are wonderful. But in no respect do they compare with responsibility and character. In these, your son is sorely lacking. Please, Sir, go about your business. Allow John to reckon with the consequences of his actions."

"Philip, I beg you to reconsider," Newton begged.

But the captain's mind was made up. "Good day, Sir."

The next day, two seamen pulled John cursing and fighting from the ship's dank prison. When he refused to walk, they shoved him up the ladder and onto the deck where the entire crew was standing at attention. Seething with hatred, John glared around until he caught sight of Lieutenant Mitchell and Job Lewis, side by side. Mitchell stared straight ahead, his face set. But Lewis was the picture of misery.

"John Newton, stand forward!" Captain Cartaret ordered.

Two seamen ripped John's jacket and shirt from his back, then they yanked off his breeches. They pushed him to the upright grate and two others bound his feet. Rebellion flaming in his eyes, John stiffened and twisted his mouth into an ugly sneer. The seamen forced him over the grating and lashed his wrists. There John hung spread-eagle.

"For desertion from His Majesty's Ship *Harwich* in time of war, I sentence John Newton to seventy-five lashes with the cat-o'-nine-tails," Captain Cartaret intoned. To John he said, "May God have mercy on your soul."

The master-at-arms stepped forward. Grasping the cat with both hands, he lifted it high over his head, swished it through the air, and, as the drum rolled, he lashed it across John's bare back. John's face twisted with pain, yet he refused to cry out. Then the second lash . . . and the third . . . and the fourth. By the fifth lash, his blood flying, John hissed curses through clenched teeth. Job squeezed his eyes shut, but Lieutenant Mitchell stared straight ahead, stone-faced. Old Hank didn't attempt to hide his tears. By lash number eight, John was groaning in agony, his face distorted with pain. Still he refused to cry out. By lash number ten, John slumped to his knees on the bloody deck. After fifteen lashes, the captain motioned the master-at-arms to halt.

"John Newton," Captain Cartaret said. "Will you beg for mercy from me and from God?"

With great effort, John forced his body upright. Holding his head erect, he strained to look the captain in the face. Then, with hate and disdain, he spat blood at him.

"Very well," the captain said. "Commence with the punishment."

In a dizzying blur of drum rolls and shouted curses, the cat flayed John's back, muscle from bone. His curses grew weaker and weaker, until finally John slumped over the grating, silent. By the time the captain finally called a halt, no one believed there was life left in John Newton.

"I *will have* discipline aboard my ship," Captain Cartaret declared. "Dismissed."

The crew beat a hasty retreat. The ship's surgeon loosened John's bonds, and, although he could see no realistic reason to do so, poured a bucket of salt water over his shredded back. Shaking his head, the surgeon wandered to the stern to clear his head.

Alone in the gathering dusk, John twitched, then he began to move. Grabbing hold of the grating, he tried to pull himself up, but the metal was too slippery with his blood. His face twisted in pain and hatred, John raised his fist to heaven, and spat out, "There . . . is . . . no . . . God!" Then he slumped back onto the deck.

✦

When John awoke, he lay in a stinking bunk in the airless below decks. He shook his head in an effort to remember. Where was he? What happened? John started to sit up, but crying out in agony, he fell back. From somewhere port side, he heard a wicked laugh. Painfully, he turned his head toward it.

"Wot's the matter?" seaman Billy Green, chortled. "Don't like yer new digs?"

John looked around in confusion. Where was he?

"Ye is a ordinary seaman agin. I's superior to ye!" Then with great laughter, Billy announced, "Don't fergit to call me Sir! And most ever'one else, too. Ye's low man now, Newton."

Stripped of his rank and back in his old quarters, John Newton was among the men he had so enjoyed bullying and abusing. Little wonder they now treated him with ridicule and scorn. As for his former mates among the officers, the captain forbade them to speak to him—even if they had the desire to do so. No more discussing philosophy. No more sitting on the deck watching the moon and tracing constellations.

As soon as he could stand, John was ordered to the deck and, despite his racking pain, was put to work at the most undesirable jobs. As John knelt sanding his own blood from the deck, Billy Green sauntered by and kicked over his bucket of soapy water. John jumped up, his fists clenched.

"Watch it, you clumsy oaf, or I'll smash your face in!"

"Sorry, Sir!" Billy replied in greatly exaggerated remorse. Then, slapping his forehead, he loudly exclaimed, "Oh, right! Ye's no sir. Now ye's jest like me."

With that, he kicked over a second bucket, then swaggered off, roaring with laughter. Lieutenant Brant, who had been watching, laughed right along with Billy.

John fumed helplessly. Insults . . . hardship . . . and absolutely no hope of relief. Bitter rage boiled up into black despair. His back began to heal, but his pride did not. Worst of all, he was certain that Mary would hear about what happened, and then she would have nothing to do with him. Certainly her parents wouldn't let

The Life of John Newton

him get close enough to explain. His life was destroyed. And it was all Captain Carteret's fault!

"I'm going to kill that *%@! captain!" John hissed under his breath.

"What'll that git ye? Keelhauled and hung out to dry?" It was Hank, and instead of the usual ridicule and sarcasm, he spoke with compassion.

"I'd rather be at the bottom of the sea than on this *#&* of a ship," John responded.

"And yer lass? What would she think of ye then?" Hank asked.

For the first time, John's eyes filled with tears. He couldn't bear to have Mary think badly of him after he was dead.

"Ye may not believe in God, but someone was lookin' out fer ye," Hank said. "Cap'n should've hung ye from the yardarm."

John stopped sanding and sat back on his heels. Looking Hank in the face he asked, "Why do you speak to me? You, of all people?"

"Why didn't ye kill me?" Hank asked in reply. "Then I couldn't sound the alarm."

On April 14, 1745, the fleet finally set sail from Plymouth Sound. Rounding Lizard Point in Cornwall next day, John caught his last glimpse of the English coastline.

"Jump!" John breathed as he gazed into the rushing sea. "Jump and have it done with."

## CHAPTER 9

# 1745

*"I cannot express with what wishfulness and regret I cast my last look upon the English shore. I kept my eyes on it until it disappeared. When I could see it no longer, I was tempted to throw myself into the sea. But the hand of God restrained me."*

BOISTEROUS LAUGHTER, PUNCTUATED BY RAUCOUS CHEERS AND HOOTS, bellowed over from starboard. John Newton, repairing halyards port side, could not contain his curiosity. He jumped up onto a stack of crates and stretched tall, yet all he could see was a crowd of sailors pushed up against the rail. And although he made it a stubborn practice to keep aloof from the other sailors, this uncommon commotion got the better of him.

John sauntered over and found James Mitchell and Job Lewis standing off to one side—James laughing and cheering, Job distinctly uncomfortable. Still unable to see over the heads in front, John worked aft—downwind.

"Whew! What is that stink?" he exclaimed.

"Slave ship passing by," said Hank.

John craned to see.

"Over 'ere," Hank called, pushing his way to the far end of the crowd.

As John shoved forward, haunting strains from a bagpipe

floated over the water. A laughing cheer arose from the men in front. At the rail, John forced his way between Hank and Manning. The passing ship was so close he could see the men on deck. A huge group of Africans, it was, chained together at their ankles. All jumping furiously about. "What in the devil's name are they doing?" John demanded.

"Dancin' one o' their heathen dances," Manning answered.

"Nah," said Hank. "Crew's exercising 'em. That's valuable cargo they got there."

"Hmmm," John mused. "Strange way to treat valuable cargo. Seems to me those chains would rub their ankles raw."

Hank shook his head. "They's no accountin' fer slavers," he said.

As the *Harwich* sailors watched, the ship's hatch opened and several seamen struggled up from below carrying Africans. One by one, they lugged them to the railing and tossed them overboard.

"Dumpin' the dead 'uns," said Hank. "Gots to do it ever day. They dies that fast."

"Won't stink so bad tonight," Manning allowed.

"'Mmmph!" Hank snorted. "Ain't never goin' to git the smell out of that ship."

An unsettling eeriness enveloped the *Harwich* as the sailors watched the slave ship sail past and out of sight.

"You men might die on a man-of-war, but at least it's an honorable death," Lieutenant Mitchell stated. "There's nothing honorable about a slave ship."

"Worse thing sailin' the seas," Hank growled. "'Cept maybe a ship gone pirate. And they's those would argue that."

In order to prepare for the long voyage to the Cape of Good Hope, the *HMS Harwich* anchored at Madeira, Spain. The May sun rose early and shone hot throughout the long day. John worked at resealing the ship's hull, laboring over bubbling caldrons of tar from dawn until the sun set. Day after day, the sun baked his still-raw back until he was nothing but a mass of blisters. Just when John thought things could get no worse, the order came to repack the ship. This meant hoisting heavy canvas sacks up over his blistered shoulders, then wooden crates and rough barrels onto his raw back.

At last Captain Cartaret announced, "The wind stands fair. We sail at dawn." But John's relief was short-lived. In the steamy heat, food quickly turned rancid and the water stagnant. The hard tack—their main staple—was so full of maggots the men had to bang the biscuits on the floor to force the bugs out. Disease swept the ship, felling man after man. All John could think was, "Lucky *&*%, getting out of here!"

The longer the stretch of days . . . the more painful his raw back . . . the more commands barked at him . . . the sicker men got on spoiled food . . . then the more bitterly enraged John grew. And the more he turned his black despair onto anyone unfortunate enough to be near him. Cursing non-stop, John plunged headlong into raging blasphemy.

"Swear if ye wants," the seamen whispered among themselves. "But blaspheme God? No! He's all that stands 'tween us and the bottom of the sea."

Officers were growing uncomfortable, too. Including the captain. Philip Cartaret was known to be a fair man, but as the voyage progressed and John's mood grew more foul, the captain's resentment swelled to insatiable.

✦

After an especially long day, John slept so soundly he didn't hear the drum roll calling all hands to deck. Not just him, either. In fact, the Masters Mate sent Job Lewis below deck to rouse all who overslept. Job kicked a hammock here and another there. When he came to John's hammock, instead of a kick, he pulled out his knife. With one quick jerk of his wrist, he sliced the ropes, dumping John to the deck. John landed with a thud on the painful sores of his back.

Immediately John was on his feet, roaring like a wounded bear. "What in the devil's holy name are you doing, you *%$*# idiot!" he bellowed. "I ought to—"

"What you ought to do," Job replied evenly, "is shut your mouth and get up on deck with everyone else. You're late."

"Couldn't you just call me?" John demanded.

"I could," Job answered. "But this got you up faster. It also gave me a good laugh." As Job strode out, other tardy seamen snickered. Some laughed out loud.

Still fuming, John took his place on deck. But a tender boat tied up alongside the *Harwich* quickly grabbed his attention. Two sailors—obviously not Royal Navy—scrambled up the ladder. John edged over to Lieutenant Mitchell.

"What's going on?" he asked. ". . . Sir?"

"Taking on a couple of merchant seamen," Mitchell said with an air of condescension. "Making up for the ones we lost. New lads for you to drive to distraction."

John knew the routine. The Royal Navy could demand any crew member it needed. It couldn't, however, leave a merchant ship undermanned. Surely if Captain Cartaret was pressing men, that captain would order an exchange.

"Exchange already made, then?" John asked as casually as possible.

Lieutenant Mitchell's eyes narrowed. "Captain is demanding two of our sailors, but the captain has only given one. Frank Sullivan—the man with the bad cough."

At this, John's haughtiness crumbled. "Please, James," he pleaded, "ask the captain to send me. I'm begging you."

Mitchell stared at him in amazement.

"Please . . . Sir. For all the times we had before. For the rational thinking we enjoyed together. Please, make it possible for me to be that second man. Please!"

For several minutes, Mitchell silently studied John.

"I'm begging you, James!"

Without a word, Lieutenant Mitchell turned and walked away.

Exchanges offered an opportunity to rid a ship of unskilled men. Or those too ill to work. It made no sense to exchange a desirable sailor. Yet, less than half an hour after Job Lewis cut John's hammock, John clambered down the ladder and boarded the *Levant*.

"Welcome aboard. I'm Captain James Phelps," said the first man to greet the new sailors. "Your names for the ship's books?"

"Frank Sullivan, Sir."

"John Newton, Sir."

At the name of John Newton, Captain Phelps perked up. "Newton, you say? Why, I do believe I know your father!" Ignoring Frank, he clapped John on the back as though they were already old friends. "We're going to get along fine, my lad. Just fine!"

"I've sailed many a merchant ship with my father," John informed his new captain. "Where are we headed?"

"Windward coast of Africa. Sierra Leone. When we're fully loaded, we sail for the West Indies."

"What's the cargo?" John asked.

"What do you think?" Captain Phelps laughed. "You're on a slaver, man! Cargo's Africans!"

Frank Sullivan's face twisted in disgust and he spat noisily onto the deck. "I should'a smelled the stink!" he growled.

For the first time, Captain Phelps looked Frank up and down. What he saw was a worn out sailor, pale and wasted, who looked as if he would be fortunate to make it to the next port. The captain sighed and shook his head.

Still, the man did have spunk. Glaring his new captain straight in the face, he pulled himself up tall and spat again. Perhaps the effect would have been stronger if Frank hadn't immediately doubled up coughing and gasping for breath.

"How about you, Newton?" the captain said, turning to John. "You one of them that thinks he's too good for a slave ship?"

"I don't care if she's gone pirate," John shot back. "I'm off the *Harwich*. That's all that matters to me."

The *Levant* sailed the triangular trade—Liverpool to Africa to the West Indies—which meant John could expect to be back home in about a year. A great cause for rejoicing. Furthermore, while at sea, John no longer need strain under such strict restraints, not from his father and not from the Royal Navy. Which meant he could abandon himself to whatever temptations might attract him. He could act exactly as he pleased.

Sam Miller, assigned the job of familiarizing newcomers with the ship, stepped forward to make John's acquaintance. The deck, masts and rigging, John recognized. Same three-masted merchant ship on which he'd sailed many times before. Nothing new, bow to stern. Then Sam opened the hatch and climbed down the ladder into the hold. John followed, with Frank right behind.

"Cargo of guns and gunpowder now, and bales of wool and

cloth," Sam said. "But once we get to Africa, we'll load up right full." He lit a lantern and held it high.

John had spent a good part of his life aboard ships. Various types and sizes, but never one like this. The hold looked to be divided into flat wooden shelves. Examining the strange configuration, John reached up to touch the heavy chains that hung from overhead. When he stepped forward in the semi-darkness, he stumbled on an iron shackle—one of many driven into the heavy timbers of the ship's main frame. Leg-irons, too, bolted into the deck. As the ship shifted, the chains clanked an eerie rhythm.

"This is a *&%# stinking prison!" John exclaimed.

"No stink to it," Sam responded. "We cleaned the *Levant* thoroughly after the last trip. And I dare say, you will be thankful enough for this prison when the Africans are loaded on. They'd as soon kill you as look at you."

"Can't say as I blame 'em," Frank mumbled.

"You better watch that mouth of yours, mate!" Sam snapped. "That's dangerous talk on a slaver."

"How many can you stow here?" John asked Sam.

"Tight pack, over four hundred," Sam said. " 'Course some will die on the way. Always do. But then, that's the business. We plan on losing about 20 percent."

"It's a ship of damnation is what it is!" Frank mumbled.

Sam laughed out loud. But for once, John's mouth was shut. The ship shifted against the wind, setting the chains and shackles to dancing. As they rattled rhythmically with the sway of the ship and the creaking of the timbers, a shiver ran up John's back.

# CHAPTER 10

# 1745

*"Thus occurred one of the many critical turns of my life,
in which the Lord was pleased to display his providence
and care by causing unexpected circumstances to con-
cur in almost an instant of time."*

As Frank Sullivan made his way onto the upper deck, John
swung down the rigging from his favorite place on the main yard
and landed nimbly in front of him. "Hey, Frankie!" he called. "You
still crying about crewing on a slave ship?"

"Shut your lip!" Frank growled.

"You think the captain's a devil-spawned pirate or
something?"

Fire flamed in Frank's eyes as he hissed, "If anyone's devil-
spawned, it's you, John Newton."

Throwing his head back, John laughed long and hard. He
grabbed up the outhaul line and tossed it at Frank, knocking him
off his feet. "Wake up!" John called. "And maybe someday you
might grow up to be a *real* sailor!"

Practically doubled over with laughter, John failed to notice
another sailor watching him. So it came as a bit of a shock when
Caleb Sneed sat beside him at supper and said, "I'd think twice
before I called anyone 'devil-spawned.'"

"You would, would you?" John answered. "I'll keep that in

mind." He shoved a bite of stew into his mouth. "You a religious man?"

"I guess you'd say so," Caleb said. "I have a healthy respect for sacred things."

"Well, now, you and I are alike in that," John told him. "I have a healthy respect for the Father, Son, and the holy devil-spawned captain!"

Caleb's face went pale as John roared with laughter.

Not that John had anything against Captain Phelps. He simply hated to obey. Even a person who granted him privileges and promised to introduce him to a new life of adventure and riches. It was Captain Phelps, after all, who had told John, "Don't let the clank of iron chains spook you, Lad. Think of it as the sound of gold coins!"

Although John knew Liverpool harbor well, he'd had little contact with any of the five thousand or so slave ships leaving each year for Africa, and none with slavers sailing from Spain, Portugal, France, or the Netherlands. He had no idea how many millions of Africans had been enslaved by the trade. Not that he could be blamed for his ignorance. No one knew how many men, women, and children had been kidnapped and shipped away to slave markets in the Americas. Certainly no one kept count of the number who perished enroute.

"Murderers, the whole lot!" That's how Frank summed up the slave trade.

Captain Phelps' simply replied, "Tell that to the honest merchants who own this ship. It's business, man. Honest business. Do your job, and thank God you're up here on the top deck."

Phelps was right, of course. Legitimate merchants did own the slave ships, and they operated them as legal businesses. Commerce fueled the entire operation. The Americas supplied cotton, sugar, and coffee to Europe, but they couldn't produce those goods without cheap human labor. It was all business, and all legal.

In the quiet of twilight, John settled himself in the ship's bow and stared out at the calm sea that stretched before him. Soon the moon would rise and the stars would appear. From his jacket he took paper, pen, and bottle of ink, and in the waning light he carefully wrote: "Dear Mary, I'm sorry I was not able to express to you the things that were on my mind. I don't know how long it will be before I see you again, but I promise I will be back. The time will be much shorter than I feared. Yours always, John Newton."

Carefully John blotted the ink with his sleeve, then he folded the paper and tucked it in his jacket. Sweet Mary . . . Polly. So very far away.

✛

As the weeks passed, John's stories grew bolder and more blasphemous. That they so unsettled the captain only encouraged John to be more and more outrageous. "I say God had lots of contests with Satan," he proclaimed one day to a group of men. "We only know about the one with Job because that's the only one God won!"

That got the sailors' attention. Several laughed. A few shouted their agreement.

"I mean, look at me. Those two have battled for my soul since I was six years old. Who would you say won?"

"Satan!" the men yelled laughing.

Besides the crew, the *Levant* had a passenger on board, a man even the captain treated with great respect. Each morning, after bathing, shaving, and trimming his moustache, the man dressed in a freshly pressed linen suit and strolled two times around the upper deck. The rest of the day he kept to himself. But he watched.

And John's high spirits amused him greatly. "Intelligent lad," he murmured to himself.

Captain Phelps didn't share that enthusiasm. John Newton's behavior failed to please him one little bit, and the captain's actions toward his once favorite hand changed dramatically. But laying the blame back on the captain, John merely heightened his blasphemy and aimed more and sharper barbs at Phelps. Finally the captain confronted John, "I'm surprised and disappointed by your attitude and behavior. Your father is a decent man and a responsible seaman. Never did I imagine he could have a son as disobedient and foul-mouthed as you. How disappointed he must be."

How dare the captain insult him! John's response was to make up a song ridiculing Phelps—his person, his motives, his running of the ship. After treating the crew to stolen rum, John taught them the song, then he led them in singing it at the top of their voices. For the next six months, he revised and improved his song, each time making it a bit more sarcastic and a whole lot more obscene. Gleefully the crew took it up, singing it over and over, reducing Captain Phelps to a laughingstock on his own ship.

As for John, he worked only when it pleased him. Disobedience, it seemed, was his special pleasure. So pointed did his criticism of the captain grow that he came close to rousing the men to mutiny. But that was just a sideline. John set his sights on an even greater project—destroying Caleb's faith. Just as he had done with Job Lewis.

One day, John stood at the ship's helm in high seas with Caleb beside him. Gigantic waves thundered into the ship, lifting it high on the crest, then plunging it down and pitching it forward. Caleb gasped and cowered, but not John. "I've been the best God-fearing child that ever was, and I've been the most debauched son of a &*#!," John said. "And I'm here to tell you, Caleb, the latter is much more fun!"

"But what if you're wrong?" Caleb asked. "What if there is a God?"

John rolled his eyes and shook his head. "A mature, rational adult like you? Isn't it time you throw out that foolishness, and all the fear of hell-fires that goes with it? You are the captain of your soul, Caleb Sneed, just like I am the captain of mine!"

At that moment, Captain Phelps was in his cabin, massaging his throbbing head. "He's trouble!" Sam Miller insisted to him. "How can you allow such disrespect?"

"He's a good sailor," Phelps replied wearily. "Much smarter than the other blokes on this ship. Better worker, too . . . when he chooses to work. We need him."

Before long, Caleb Sneed was constantly at John's side. "See, the important thing is to let everyone know who's in charge," John instructed his protégé as they swaggered across the deck.

"What do you mean?" Caleb asked.

John pointed to Captain Phelps. "He thinks he's the boss, but I'm really the one in charge here."

Caleb laughed out loud. "You aren't in charge of anything!"

"No?" John challenged. "Meet me right here tonight, middle watch."

Caleb arrived at four bells in the middle watch—two o'clock in the morning. Slurred voices echoed from behind a pile of barrels, punctuated with periodic warnings of "shush." Laughter, too, and clinking bottles. Rounding the corner he saw a dozen merry sailors clustered around John, all drinking heartily from a cask of rum. Caleb rushed to join the fun. Raising his mug, he cried, "To John Newton!"

"To John Newton!" echoed a dozen drunken voices.

John, completely sober, raised an empty mug and proclaimed, "To Captain Phelps who generously opened his liquor cabinet for our enjoyment. . . . Not that he knows it yet." He thrust a ring of keys high into the air and swung them around triumphantly as the men broke into wild guffaws.

"Where'd you get those?" Caleb asked.

With a wink and a wicked grin, John said, "Gain their trust and you're in charge. Mark it down in your lesson book, my lad!"

The next morning Sam Miller approached John as he worked on the standing rigging. "The men are quiet today," he announced.

John stopped his work. In an exaggerated manner, he shaded his eyes and gazed up at the sun, then across the deck to the passenger watching them, then out at the expanse of ocean. "Well, now, nothing like a beautiful morning to set a body to meditating."

"I'm thinking they're hung over."

John, affecting great shock, exclaimed, "What would give you such an idea?"

"The captain's liquor cabinet is empty."

"Hmmm," said John. "Sure it's not the captain who's hung over?"

Seething, Sam threatened, "One of these days you're going to go too far!"

John opened his eyes wide with innocence and exclaimed, "Why, Sir, I'm going to Africa. Is that too far?"

Sputtering with rage, Sam started to answer back, then stormed off. John looked over at Caleb and grinned broadly. "Let them know who's in charge, my lad," he called.

Chuckling to himself, the passenger stood up and headed back to his cabin.

Later that evening, while the men awaited their dinner, John jumped up on a table and set them to laughing with his brand of entertainment. ". . . So the fool of a captain says to St. Peter, 'I want the keys to heaven's liquor cabinet!' And St. Peter says—"

Sam Miller stumbled through the doorway, his face ashen. "Captain Phelps is burning with fever. I don't think he'll live through the night." Pointing to John, Sam said, "He warned you, John Newton. He told you your blasphemy would bring God's wrath down on us!"

"Really?" John asked sarcastically. "The God of the universe has nothing better to do?" He threw his head back and hooted. But not one man joined him. Frank Sullivan spat in disgust and walked out.

✦

The next morning, with the entire *Levant* crew standing at attention, Sam Miller intoned, "We commit Captain James Phelps to the sea. May he rest in peace." After the burial at sea, Sam stated, "This ship is now under my command. Make no mistake, I am not Captain Phelps. Things *will* be different. You are dismissed."

John turned to leave with the others, but Sam stopped him. "I repeat, I am *not* James Phelps. Keep up your foolishness and I will hand you back to the *Harwich*. With my personal condolences to them."

As John headed below deck, the gentleman who had watched him throughout the voyage fell in step beside him. "Excuse me, Sir," he said. "I couldn't help observing you over these past weeks. Forgive me for being so bold, but it would seem that you are not . . . can we say . . . a favorite of the new captain."

"I think we can say that," John said.

"Allow me to introduce myself. The name's Clow, and I'm a businessman on the Guinea coast. I have a proposition to lay before you." Clow put his arm around John's shoulder, and the two walked on. For once John was listening instead of talking.

# CHAPTER 11

# 1745

*"I was about to reap a terrible harvest of misery and wrong."*

AFRICA! JOHN LEANED OUT OVER THE SHIP'S RAILING AND BREATHED IN the smells of a new land—spices . . . exotic animals . . . sun-baked earth. Alluring fragrances of excitement and endless possibilities.

Most often, ships sailing to West Africa anchored off-shore where captains could watch for tell-tale smoke signals from resident slave dealers signifying that they had captives for sale. Not Sam Miller, however. So eager was he to be rid of John Newton that he maneuvered past the waiting ships and dropped anchor right alongside the empty gangway. As the crew set to work unloading boxes of cargo, John slung his sack over his shoulder and swaggered toward the gangplank.

"Good riddance!" Sam snapped. "You're a blight on humanity!"

John laughed. "You'll still be commanding this worthless tub, while I'm swimming in riches."

"Bah!" Sam shot back. "It's enough to have you off my ship and out of my sight."

"John!" Caleb called. John didn't slow his pace, he didn't speed up, either. When Caleb caught up to him, he pleaded, "What will I do without you?"

"Caleb! Caleb!" John said with a wink and a grin. "I've taught you well. Just remember, be sure Miller knows who's in charge."

And so, with little more than the clothes on his back and without a glance behind him, John crossed the gangplank to begin life in Africa.

"So, what exactly is your job?" John asked Clow.

"Why, to count the gold pouring into my coffers," Clow replied. "And to rule over my islands. And to run my business . . . which is one of the most profitable slave islands in this area. And you, my lad, will be my assistant."

By the mid-eighteenth century, the slave trade had begun to take its toll on Africa's coast. With most potential slaves already carried away, necessity drove slave catchers farther and farther into the interior. Not that it was a big problem. Plenty of enterprising Africans were all too willing to raid villages of enemy tribes and drag captives back to the coast where they could trade them for guns and gunpowder, or even for cloth or pots or rum. Which is why British ship owners decided it made sense to have British representatives positioned in Africa, available to buy the best captives as they arrived at the coast. These buyers imprisoned the terrified Africans in locked pens until an appropriate ship arrived to take them away from Africa forever. For the British, the system worked well. Ships spent far less time off the African coast.

Not only was Clow one of the British middle men, he was one of the most powerful, wealthy, and independent of them. All traits John admired.

*When I'm a successful slave trader like Clow . . .* John imaged wistfully . . . *No! When I'm much greater than Clow! . . . then we'll see what my father has to say about my reputation and responsibility. I'll sail back to England a wealthy man, and Mary's father will beg me to marry his daughter. And she will be so glad she waited for me. Nothing but riches and happiness. At last, all my dreams coming true. . . .*

The multitude of rivers lacing the African coast—many small and completely unnavigable—were inhabited by a plethora of creatures unknown in Europe, and they swarmed with disease-bearing mosquitoes. One of the navigable rivers was the Sierra Leone, and approximately twelve leagues southeast of it lay three islands known as the Benanoes. Most of the area's white men lived there. But seven leagues farther, alongside the Sherbro River, lay the three small Plantane Islands. Clow and John rowed to the largest of these, then pulled their boat up on the beach.

"We begin building tomorrow," Clow told John. "I hope to start trading from this island before too many weeks pass."

*Hardly likely*, John thought as he looked at the sandy island stretched out before him. Almost totally covered with coconut groves and banana trees, it wasn't much to look at—no hills or winding rivers. Not even a waterfall. Still, as Clow pointed out, water surrounded the two-mile-long island, which made it an ideal anchorage. Perfect for landing shallops—the small boats that would bring slaves down the nearby rivers—yet easy for European ships to spot. Secure, too. Slaves could be set to work with no fear of escape, since the only way out was by boat, and even that required an experienced sailor able to navigate the reefs.

"See the cove?" Clow asked. "Faces northeast. With its sloping beach and the trees, it makes a natural protection against the winds that roar through here. Also—"

"What the #*@ . . . !" John jumped back as a snake slithered past him.

"Oh, I should mention," Clow said, "the island is crawling with snakes." Didn't seem to bother him, though, since he went right on talking. "Right now, there's only my house. But we'll put a large warehouse over there, and on that side huts for the slaves who work the plantation. And off to that side a huge holding area. That's where we'll hold the Africans for the slave ships."

"Sounds like you have it all planned out," John said.

"Oh, yes!" Clow answered. "All I needed was someone like you." Then he pointed to a flat area not far from the beach. "We'll build you a house there. Then we'll get started on clearing out these coconuts before we leave for a trip inland."

"Why take out the coconut trees?" John asked.

"Got plenty on my other islands," Clow said. "Here, I want to plant limes."

"Limes!" John exclaimed. "Who wants limes?"

"Only every ship's captain with a brain in his head. Ever see a man dying with scurvy? It's limes that will cure it. If a ship's got scurvy, the captain will pay me any price I ask. Limes will make me rich."

Clow led John up to his house, pausing to show off the surrounding garden filled with pumpkins, watermelons, squash, pineapples, and paw-paws. "I have a separate cook room out back," he said, "and a good-sized storehouse, too." Then he called out, "Pae'ai! Where are you, woman?"

A tall, exquisite African woman rushed out of the house, all smiles, and ran toward Clow. John was taken aback by her beauty and charm. Flamboyantly dressed in European clothes, she was adorned in heavy gold jewelry from her head piece right down to her toe rings. Clow, however, never glanced at her. Instead he threw his arm around John's shoulders and led him into the house. "Got me an assistant here," he announced. "Name's John Newton. You'll be seeing a lot of him."

Pae'ai stopped still and her smile faded.

"She's a good woman," Clow confided to John. "A princess. Nothing but the best for Clow!"

Suddenly realizing she wasn't with them, Clow bellowed, "Woman! Where's our food? You've got two hungry men here, and we don't want to wait!"

As Pae'ai walked through the house to the kitchen out back, she shot John a withering look. Clow, taking no notice, led John into a room elaborately set with European china and silverware. Black slaves stood by ready to serve.

"I don't think your woman is too happy to have me here," John commented.

"Just a touch jealous," Clow said. "Does her good to be kept in her place."

"She your wife?"

"Goodness, no!" Clow said with a laugh. "I've got more sense than to marry an African. But she's as good as a wife, if you know what I mean." He winked and nudged John. "Got influence out here, too, which doesn't hurt me none."

Quite true. In fact, Pae'ai's father controlled most of the village raiding in the area. And Pae'ai was a woman of such great importance in her country that Clow owed a great deal of his position and fortune to her and her wise decision-making.

"Maybe she'd feel better about me if I had a woman of my own," John suggested.

"Well, now, maybe she would," Clow said. "We'll find you one tomorrow . . . Which reminds me, I have letters for you. Miller gave them to me when I left the ship."

"He held back my letters? Why, that devil *!#* . . . !"

"Some have awfully pretty writing," Clow said, laughing as he pulled out the stack and handed them over.

✦

It didn't take long to construct John's house of coconut logs and to thatch the roof with banana leaves. By late afternoon he was able to spread a mat on the floor, then stretch out, and tear open the first letter addressed in Mary's hand:

"Dear John, I felt I must write and encourage you on your long voyage. I can't imagine what it's like to look out at God's creation all day long. Please know I am praying for your safe return to London. Your friend, Mary Catlett."

He thumbed past two from his father and found another from Mary:

"Dear John, It's raining here today. I wonder what kind of weather you must endure. I am praying to God to bring you safely home. Faithfully yours, Mary Catlett."

Rather than speaking of the weather or God's creation, the letter John wrote back to Mary boasted of the wealth and power soon to be his.

✦

Day after day, Clow supervised the slaves who struggled to uproot and remove the coconut trees. John followed along behind planting lime trees. Late one afternoon, when John paused to wipe his face and catch his breath, he said, "Tell me about our trip."

"We'll load up the boats with guns and rum and trinkets to trade, then head up the Rio Nunez to the trader villages," Clow told him. "When we've purchased as many Africans as the boats will hold, we'll bring them back here to wait for the trading ships. I only take the best, and I only sell them for gold."

"Gold! Now that sounds like a proper business!"

"So," Clow said with a broad grin, "gold sets your conscience aright, does it?"

"That and a good-looking woman of my own."

Laughing heartily, Clow clapped John on the back. "You and me are going to get along just fine, lad. Just fine!"

It took several months to get the land cleared, lime trees planted, and the buildings built. But finally Clow announced that they would leave the next day at dawn. "Be at the boats early to help me finish packing," he instructed.

The next morning, the sun already full in the sky, Clow loaded the last of the supplies into the boats . . . alone . . . as Pae'ai watched from the house. The very idea of her self-satisfied I-told-you-so look filled him with rage. Striding up to John's door, Clow bellowed, "Where are you? I said sun up!" When John didn't answer, he kicked the door open. John lay on the mat, moaning with delirium and drenched with sweat.

Back at the big house, Clow paced the floor, his agitation growing by the minute. "Great investment he is! Two whole months I'll be gone, and without a lick of help."

"Can't you wait until he's better?" Pae'ai asked.

Clow shook his head. "Looks of him, he might not get better. Anyway, I can't wait. I'll have to leave without him!" Then, his voice softening, he added, "Too bad, though. I will miss him. Only intelligent conversation I get in this godforsaken land!" At the doorway, Clow stopped and turned back to Pae'ai. "See that he gets his health back. When I get home, I want John well."

When Pae'ai didn't answer, Clow demanded, "Do you hear me, woman? I'm still your master!"

✦

Day after day, John lay on his mat, thrashing in the throes of hallucinations. Pae'ai stood to one side, giving instructions to the slaves who bathed his face and tried to get him to take a drink of water. One day, the slave Nhama stood helplessly by with a bowl of broth as John, soaked with sweat and barely conscious, gasped for breath.

"Give that to me!" Pae'ai ordered. Grabbing the bowl, she tried to force John to drink. But after only a few swallows, he choked and fell back on his mat.

"He's not even trying!" Pae'ai declared in disgust. "He just *wants* me to wait on him. Well, he can wait on himself!" She thrust the bowl at Nhama and marched out. But before hurrying after her, Nhama set the bowl down close to the mat where John could reach it.

When John finally opened his eyes, he was alone. His pillow had been replaced with a log of wood. So weak he could hardly move, John licked his parched lips. Then, spying the bowl of cold broth, he mustered all his strength and struggled to reach it . . . only to knock it over and spill it across the floor. Frantically, he fell onto the puddle and desperately licked it up. Then, totally exhausted, he flopped back onto the mat.

Quite a different story up in the big house. There Pae'ai, surrounded by the greatest of European luxuries—courtesy of visiting ships' captains—enjoyed a most sumptuous meal elegantly served by attentive slaves.

"Bindo!" Pae'ai called out to a muscle-bound slave. "Is John Newton dead yet?"

"No, Madame," Bindo answered.

"Why not?!" Pae'ai demanded. She looked at Nhama. "Are you feeding him?"

"No, Madame," Nhama said.

"Forgive me, Madame," Bindo said in a low, rumbling voice. "Master say he must live. How do he live if he not eat?"

Pae'ai's eyes narrowed. "Have you been feeding him, Bindo?"

"Master tell you to care for him, Madame."

"I am queen of this Island, and you'll do things my way now!" Pae'ai raged. "Clow isn't here, so I'm the master. You call me master!"

"Yes, Master," Bindo rumbled.

Pae'ai studied the scraps on her plate. The best of them, she picked out and threw to the dog who lay at her feet. Then she pushed the rest into a pile—the fish heads and bones, the yam skins and corn husks—and she handed her plate to Bindo. "Here. Take this to that wretch. Tell him dinner is with my compliments."

After weeks of a raging fever, John desired food and was desperate for water. He could hardly raise his head from the wooden pillow. Now and then, one or another of the slaves, leg-chains clanging, dared sneak something to him. Late one afternoon, Nhama crept into John's house carrying a gourd of water and a bowl of boiled roots. John grabbed the water and drank it to the bottom.

"Bring me more!" John begged.

But Nhama, startled by rustling outside the door, quickly scooped up the empty gourd and slipped out, leaving the boiled roots behind.

Weeks later, as Pae'ai enjoyed yet another lavish meal, she stopped in mid-bite to demand, "Bindo! Does John Newton still live?"

"Yes, Master."

Sighing in exasperation, she ordered, "Bring him here." When no one moved, she added, "Now!"

The sun was beginning to set as John slowly staggered toward the big house, hanging onto the fence for support. Pae'ai, still eating, didn't bother to look up as Bindo helped him into the room. Slowly, deliberately, Pae'ai put down her fork and knife, then she looked John up and down. Absolutely pitiful he looked with filthy clothes hanging off his emaciated body.

"Well!" Pae'ai said. "You certainly don't know how to dress for dinner. I cannot have you sitting at my table looking so disgusting. You'll just have to stand there until I'm finished eating." She went back to her dinner of roast chicken, poached fish, sumptuous fruit and vegetables, fluffy rice, and wine. As she ate, she emphasized her enjoyment by smacking her lips and commenting about the delicious attributes of each food. And all the time, John watched in agony, swaying on his feet.

"Please," he dared to beg. "Just a tiny bite—"

"Wait your turn or you'll get nothing!" Pae'ai snapped. If anything, she ate more slowly than ever, noisily licking every bone and sucking the juice from every scrap.

"Oh, John," Pae'ai asked lightly, "do you like the new pillow I gave you? I thought it might give your head more support."

"Yes," John almost cried. "Thank you."

At long last, Pae'ai picked up her napkin and, in an exaggerated way, wiped her mouth. Then she handed her plate to John. Shaking with eager anticipation, he lurched forward and grabbed it.

"Thank you!" he cried. "Oh, thank you, thank you!"

But in his eagerness, he stumbled, then he fumbled, then he dropped the plate, spilling the leftovers to the floor. John fell to his hands and knees, and snatching up the pieces of food—the chicken bones, skin, and gristle, the pieces of rice, the bits of vegetable—and stuffed each into his mouth.

"Here, dog!" Pae'ai called through her laughter. "Come get the scraps!"

Quickly John crawled on all fours to her chair to snatch up the scraps. Suddenly it no longer seemed funny. Kicking at him, Pae'ai cried, "He disgusts me! Get him away!"

Bindo tried to pull him away, but John held onto the chair as he licked the floor.

"Get him out of my house!" Pae'ai shrieked.

It took the help of two more slaves to finally pry John loose.

Fortunately for John, the moon cast little light that night. He waited until the last light in the big house was doused, then he held back for what seemed another hour or so. As desperate as he was, he knew he must be extremely careful. If Pae'ai caught him, she would have him hanged as a thief. Even so, he couldn't help himself. Slowly, stealthily, he struggled to the far edges of the garden. Only cassava grew there. John quickly clawed up a few roots and stuffed them into his mouth, dirt and all. Cassava roots . . . so delicious boiled or roasted, but practically inedible raw. Still, John struggled to chew the mouthful until it finally choked him. Sinking back against a lime tree, he buried his head in his hands and wept.

The next day, all the working slaves stood bunched together in the first lime grove John had planted. Pae'ai was there too, watching impatiently as John limped slowly over from his house. "So, worthless sluggard," she called out. "Are you finally ready to pick up a hoe and do your share of the work?"

"Please, Madame—" John began.

"You will address me as Master," Pae'ai said coldly.

"Please, Master. I'm starving."

"Oh, are you?" Pae'ai mocked. "Well, we can't have that! Run right up here and get this bread." She tore off a hunk of bread and held it up. Immediately, John lunged forward. "No, no! I said *run*! If you want the bread, run up here." John, did his best, but he immediately stumbled and fell. "Why, I've never seen such running!" Pae'ai pronounced. Then she asked the slaves, "Have you?"

The slaves hesitated. Reluctantly, they shook their heads no.

"Get up and run some more," Pae'ai demanded. "We must learn your technique."

John, totally miserable, begged, "Please, I—"

"Get up and run or you will go back to your hut with no food and no water!"

John struggled to his feet and attempted a ragged running-stumble. Pae'ai roared with laughter, clapping her hands enthusiastically. "Oh, John, what a clown you are! Come, everyone, join in! See if you can be as funny as John!"

No one moved. Everyone glanced at one another for clues as to what to do.

"Run like John is running!" Pae'ai ordered. "Now!" The slaves mimicked first his run, then his falling down. When he started to cry in frustration, they mimicked that as well.

"Please," John pleaded. "Please give me some food."

"Of course," Pae'ai answered in mocking kindness. "Here is your food." She picked up a rotten tomato and threw it, hitting John squarely in the face. Laughing, she threw another, and ordered the slaves to join in. As they pelted him, John, in pitiful desperation, scrapped off the rotten food and stuffed it into his mouth. When the garbage was gone, the slaves grabbed up hard limes that had fallen off the trees and threw them. When they were gone, they threw rocks. John covered his face and cowered.

"Master, please stop," Bindo rumbled. "Mr. Master say this man to be well. He be angry if he hurt bad."

"If the slaves rise up and harm John Newton, surely I can't be held responsible," Pae'ai stated. Then with a satisfied grin, she turned and walked back to the house.

Bindo positioned himself between the slaves and John, who by now was crumpled on the ground, sobbing. Raising his hands,

Bindo ordered, "Stop! If this man dies, we be punished! We must make him well!"

CHAPTER 12

# 1745

*"There were not many crimes I could not be justly charged with. But if nothing else, I was honest."*

THIN AND FILTHY, HIS CHEEKS SUNKEN AND HIS FEET BLISTERED, JOHN dragged his body over the sand searching desperately for something he could eat. Food . . . it was all he thought about. Now and then, when a ship came close to shore, he would scurry into a grove of trees and hide until it left. Humiliation and shame kept him from letting anyone see what he had become. Yet, he did have a remnant of pride left. In the dark of night he struggled to the water, took off his only shirt and washed it on the rocks. Then he put it back on wet.

One evening, after he had foraged unsuccessfully for food, John propped himself up in his house. He took a paper, pen, and ink from his sack, and carefully wrote: "Dear Father, I am writing to implore you to help me if you can. I am being held a captive at the Plantane Islands off Sierra Leone. Please help me soon or I may not live to see you again. Your desperate son, John."

Then, his hands shaking, he took out another piece of paper and hesitantly began to write again: "Dear Mary, Thank you for the letters. It lifts my spirits to hear from you. Please do not stop writing to me. Sometimes I feel so terribly alone. I don't suppose you can imagine with all your family and friends around you. Your friend forever, John Newton."

He folded both letters, then tucked them away inside his shirt.

The next morning, as John started on his foraging rounds, a wonderful sight greeted him: Clow was pulling his fully laden boat up into the cove. As the slaves ran to help him, John stumbled down to the beach. "You're back!" he called. "I didn't think I'd live to see this day."

"Well, I'm glad to see you're still alive," Clow said. "Looks like Pae'ai did a good job of nursing you."

"Nursing me?! That woman of yours would have liked to killed me! She tried to starve me to death! And even that wasn't enough for her. Why, she actually—" and John rushed into his entire sorry tale. ". . . And if it weren't for a handful of slaves who risked their own wellbeing to help me, I would be a dead man today."

"Well, now, I find this whole story impossible to believe," Clow said, shaking his head incredulously. "You'll understand if I ask my woman to tell me her side."

"She'll never admit to what she did!" John protested.

"I think I know her well enough to get to the bottom of this."

Pae'ai was ready. As Clow headed up the road, before he even had a chance to ask, she started in on her side of the story. And the more she talked, the angrier she grew. ". . . If he had his way, he would lie around on that mat all day like he was master and I was his slave. He is lazy and arrogant, and you cannot believe one word that comes out of his mouth! And—"

Finally Clow broke in and said, "Even if everything you say is true, I have a lot invested in him. I'll take him upriver with me and you won't be bothered."

The following week, Clow led upriver in the larger of two shallops—a light two-masted craft with a small cabin below—and John followed in another. As the river wound farther inland into the thick jungle overgrowth, slaves moved the boats along with long rafting poles. Once they reached the slavers' camp, Clow showed John how to mix with other traders and fight for the best deal. Captive Africans, bound hand and foot and chained at the neck, stood displayed before them. From the day of their capture deep in the African interior, and all during their long trek to the coast, the captives had worn those chains.

John watched in fascination as Clow moved among the terrified Africans, forcing mouths open and checking teeth, running his hands over naked bodies—sometimes roughly, sometimes in a manner that made John blush. "Look for good health," Clow instructed. "And good size and strength." He pointed to several Africans whose backs were crisscrossed with wounds and scars. "Defiant . . . which means dangerous," he warned. "Look at that one." Clow pointed to a badly beaten man, face set, staring straight ahead. "Whipped him to break his will. But look at his eyes . . . They failed."

Under a large baobab tree, several groups of children huddled together, attached by their necks with a rope tied from one to another. "Slavers don't waste chains on them," Clow said. "Children aren't worth enough."

One by one, Clow made his choices. Overseeers pulled the selected Africans away, though they cried and clung to those left behind. Families screamed, gripping each other until they were whipped loose and dragged off. When Clow chose a woman with a baby in her arms, an overseer grabbed her little one and dashed it to death against a tree. Horrified, John leapt at the overseer, but Clow held him back. "Had to be done, lad. It was too young to survive the trip. And the extra weight would weaken the mother."

A pair of tall, strong twins who looked to be in their late teens, caught Clow's eye. Immediately he began haggling over a purchase price. But he wasn't the only one interested in the two. Another trader, Nathan Hathaway, continually outbid him. "Does my colleague offer trinkets for such a fine matched set?" Clow asked with more than a note of sarcasm. "I've got muskets from England, and gunpowder a-plenty."

"What I'm offering is every bit as good as muskets," Hathaway countered. "Here are jewels." Hathaway laid strings of beads before the African slave catcher.

"Jewels? Ha! Nothing but glass and paste!" Clow sneered. Then to the African, "Although my price is already more than generous, I'll throw in a cask of brandy so your men can celebrate an excellent business deal."

The brandy clinched the deal. To Hathaway's consternation, the African handed the manacled twins over to Clow. As Clow and John walked away with the prize, John turned and shouted back, "Hey, old man! You can name your next purchase Jewel. We'll name these two Musket and Brandy!" To John's great pleasure—and Hathaway's deep chagrin—the other traders found the suggestion uproariously funny.

"Maybe instead of always talking, you should shut your mouth now and then," Hathaway blustered. "You might learn something."

"Yeah?" John shot back. "Maybe you could teach me how to get suckered out of two black twins at once!"

"Why you filthy little . . ." Hathaway, his fists flying, tried to jump John. But Nathan Hathaway had a bad habit of seeking solace from a rum bottle, and even in John's weakened condition, it was no contest.

"You're nothing but a fool, too stupid to be called a sailor!" John spat. He made a rude gesture, then walked away leaving Hathaway to wallow in his humiliation.

After so long a time alone, John greatly enjoyed the camaraderie of other traders. Long after Clow left to secure the day's purchases, John stayed, exchanging stories and sharing gossip. "You sailed with James Mitchell?" one asked after a chance comment about his old friend from *HMS Harwich* days. "Too bad about him. Thrown overboard in a storm off the coast of Portugal, he was. Lost at sea." As John made his way back that evening, he couldn't help wondering what Lieutenant Mitchell thought of Lord Shaftsbury's rational thought as the cold water closed over him.

"Where have you been?" Clow demanded when John finally returned to the ship.

"With the other traders," John said. "Why? What's wrong?"

"Plenty!" Clow exclaimed. "I went to pay for today's purchases and the crate of muskets isn't in the sleeping quarters! What do you know about this?"

John vehemently insisted he knew nothing of the matter. Anyway, what use had he for a box of muskets?

"Only you and I had access to our cabin," Clow said, "and I know I didn't take them. And considering their value, I'd say you have plenty of use for them."

"I am not a thief!" John proclaimed.

"Then you won't mind if I search your things, will you?"

Actually, John minded very much. How dare Clow accuse him of thievery! Yet he had no choice but to watch as Clow dumped out his belongings. Then, to John's shock—and to Clow's consternation—a pile of gold coins thunked to the floor. "What!?" John cried. "Where in the *%#!* did that come from?"

"How stupid do you think I am?" Clow said. "This is the exact worth of those stolen muskets."

Although John protested long and loud, Clow would have none of it. "And to think you accused my woman!" he raged. "I almost believed you, too! Well, now I'm stuck here with you, and believe me, I'll see that you earn your keep. But I'll never trust you again." Clow slammed the door shut and bolted it, leaving John locked alone in the shallop's cabin.

The next day, as John worked silently alongside Clow, Nathan Hathaway happened by. Unusually jolly, he called in a loud voice, "Pleasant morning to you both! And a special thanks to you, John Newton! I appreciate those muskets you sold me!"

"It was you!" John cried, bolting toward Hathaway. "You stole those muskets!" But Hathaway had already slipped into the jungle. Turning to Clow, John implored, "Don't you see? He did it to get back at me!"

"It's always someone else's fault, isn't it?" Clow replied. "Just get back to work."

"But didn't you hear what he said?"

"I'm weary of the whole matter, and I'm weary of you. Not another word."

Clow, who trusted no one, had located a mooring upstream and anchored his boats away from the other traders. "You'll stay and guard our purchases," he informed John next morning. But before he left, he wrapped a chain around John's ankle, then bolted it to the deck railing. He tossed him a bowl of rice and a container of water, then turned to go.

"Wait!" John called. "How long will you be gone?"

Clow shrugged. "Couple of days. Maybe longer."

"You can't leave me chained up all that time!" John protested. Clow kept walking. "This isn't nearly enough food!" John called. "Or water!"

That night, a tropical storm blew in, sending the boat spinning on its moorings. Sheets of rain poured down and torrential waves swept over the deck. John, chained to the rolling ship, pitched helplessly in all directions. When the storm finally passed, he huddled, soaking wet and shivering. Vainly he struggled to fight off clouds of mosquitoes intent on eating him alive. John longed for morning, yet with daybreak came the merciless sun. Blistering heat by day, and by night, violent storms and cold winds.

John's plan was to somehow make his small portion of rice last until Clow returned. But the first night's storm left the bowl lying empty on its side. Desperate with hunger, he fashioned a fish hook and, at the changing of the tides when the current was still, did his best to catch a fish. Some days he was successful. When he wasn't, he lay down and hungrily rode out the stormy night.

Periodically, Clow returned to add more slaves to the hold. At those times, John worked. But whenever Clow left, it was with John chained to the deck. The pungent stench of human misery and overflowing slop buckets reached him from below. And as the tossing, rolling ship rang with screams in many African languages, John was certain he heard the captives' praying for death. If only he could still pray. . . .

✦

After two months, Clow and John returned to the Plantanes. "I hope you are rested," Clow said, "because your days of leisure are over."

As they unloaded the new captives, Clow assigned each a number and branded each with his seal. John shaved each one's head. "Lice," Clow said. Then he warned, "Take care none escape and drown themselves. I've got good money invested here."

Once the slaves were in the holding pen, Clow and John headed out to the lime groves. The trees had grown well, and fruit was already maturing. Clow was so pleased he decided they would immediately put in another grove. If John harbored any hopes of working as an overseer, they were immediately crushed. He labored right beside the other slaves. And like them, he worked in leg-irons to prevent escape. For hours on end, John stooped over under the blazing sun, planting row upon row of tiny shoots. If he didn't work fast enough, the African overseer's lash quickly spurred him on.

John continued to scratch out an occasional letter to his father, describing his predicament, asking forgiveness, and pleading for help. These he passed on to Bindo, begging him to do his best to sneak them into Clow's mailbag.

"Speed it up, Newton!" Clow called out one day as John sagged in the relentless heat. "I want these trees in before the year's over!"

Without a word of protest, John struggled to pick up his pace. At that moment, Pae'ai happened to stroll past, and she commented on how well the planting was going.

"That's because we have the great John Newton working for us," Clow quipped. "Just look at him go!"

"He must think he's still your partner," Pae'ai said, laughing.

"Hey, John!" Clow called out. "Maybe by the time these trees grow up, you'll have gone back to England and gotten a ship of your own. Then you can come back here and help yourself to your share of the limes!"

What a great joke! Clow and Pae'ai laughed hysterically.

Day after torturous day, John's only relief was to take his treasured copy of Barrow's *Euclid* and trudge out to some remote corner of the island where, with a long stick, he drew mathematical diagrams in the sand. Cold, hungry, and wretched he may be, but he was fast becoming a master of *Euclid*'s first six books.

More than a year after John joined Clow, he was planting trees with the slaves one day when another white man pulled his boat up onto the shore. Immediately, John bolted and hid in the nearest thicket.

"Richard, my good fellow!" Clow called. "What brings you to my island?"

"Curiosity," Richard Williams answered. "What's that you're planting?"

"Limes. English sailors can't do without them. But, come now, I don't believe you came all this way to see my lime trees."

"Well, there is one other thing," Williams admitted. "I hear tell you got yourself a white slave."

Clow spat on the ground in disgust. "That I do. Though I think of him more as a servant I'm punishing. Either way, a more worthless sluggard I never did see."

Williams looked at the slaves at work, then around the grove. "Well, where is he?" he asked.

"Hiding," Clow said. "Too embarrassed to be seen. He's a strange one."

"Well, now," Williams said, "might we sit in the shade and talk man to man?"

Finally daring to emerge from his hiding place, John kept his head low as he crept back to work. He didn't see Clow approach. "Clean yourself up and come to my house," Clow ordered. "Someone wants to meet you."

When John arrived, he stayed outside, his head down and his eyes looking at the ground. "I told you he wasn't much," Clow said to Williams.

Richard Williams introduced himself to John and told him he was a trader with a number of factories and businesses across several islands. Then he asked, "Would you be willing to come and work for me?"

John jerked to attention. "Are you mocking me?" he asked.

"Certainly not! If you're willing, I'll take you with me today."

Almost afraid to hope, John looked over at Clow.

"Go!" Clow said. "But don't expect any pay from me. Not after all the trouble you've caused!"

✦

Soap and fresh water to wash . . . Clean clothes . . . A proper meal, served at a table. Ah, what luxuries! John had almost forgotten.

And respect. From the very first day, his new boss assumed John capable and intelligent, and he treated him as such. John exceeded his expectations.

Richard Williams owned five slave factories spread over a huge area, each managed by a white man. After a few months, he offered John the opportunity to take over the furthest one—along the Kittam River, almost one hundred miles away, but only a mile from the seacoast. John would work with Peter Tallison, whom he had already gotten to know and whose company he enjoyed. If all went well, Williams told John, he could have a share in the Kittam business.

Good food . . . good wages . . . women on demand . . . an amiable work situation . . . little supervision . . . a bright future . . . What more could John want? Under his careful eye, the business flourished. Life was good.

Periodically, John and Peter packed supplies into a boat and made their way to outlying villages by way of crocodile-infested rivers. Huge snakes hung from the trees overhead and swam in the water around them. Warily John eyed the lazy hippopotami—river horses, the Africans called them—as they lounged in the mud. Should one of those huge animals charge, it could easily tip their boat over.

In the villages, they would barter for ivory, gold, precious stones . . . and for slaves. Unlike many traders who took any opportunity to cheat the villagers, John always dealt honestly and fairly with them. Which was why he and Peter were always welcomed and treated like kings. It didn't hurt that the chiefs knew they had British luxuries to lavish on the village, of course. And even more, that they could provide weapons strong enough to make the chiefs rulers over their neighbors. So trusted were John and Peter that the villagers invited them to sleep in their wood and mud thatched-roof huts with them. And the village men asked them to sit and smoke pipes and drink rice wine while the women went on with their washing and cooking and planting and reaping and pounding rice into powder to make more wine for the men.

In Africa, John felt wonderfully free from the strictures of western civilization's moral codes. So whenever village chiefs offered him the pick of their women, he accepted, gratefully and gladly.

*A perfect life!* John thought, as he sat back and surveyed one African village after another. *These people are so at peace.*

Their religious beliefs also captivated John. At night, the Africans danced around a blazing fire as drums beat out a frenzied rhythm. Always one to mock superstitions, John now stood in awe of witchdoctors and totems and bad spirits. Especially drawn to rituals protecting against evil, he once witnessed the sacrifice of twin babies. ("Bad luck for the village," he was told.) A witch doctor gave John a goat-leather bag with an alligator bone inside, assuring him the talisman would ward off bad spirits. John kept the bag close to him at all times, refusing to make any important decisions without gripping it and consulting the ancestors. Once, when Peter spied a leopard lurking on the edge of the jungle, John nonchalantly commented, "Just a Bulon man." In answer to Peter's incredulous questioning, John said, "Don't you know? They change like that so they can attack men from another tribe and start a war. Gets them more slaves to sell."

Peter stopped and stared at John. "Do you really believe all that bunk?"

"Just because you don't understand doesn't mean it's bunk!"

"Listen, John, you've got a good life here. We both do. But I have to tell you, you worry me. I mean, you've gone African."

"That's crazy!" John argued.

"Yeah? Well, you just tell me one thing," Peter grabbed the goat's skin bag John wore around his neck. "Do you believe in evil spirits?"

Yanking the bag away, John stalked off without answering.

"There you are!" Peter called after him. "You *are* more African than English. You wouldn't go home if you could."

✦

Late one February afternoon in 1747, two years after John arrived in Africa aboard the *Levant,* he and Peter wound up their preparations to head inland on a trading trip. Although they were already several days late, Peter pleaded for a bit longer. They really needed a few more trade articles, so he suggested they walk along the beach on the off chance a stray merchant vessel should happen by. *Foolish idea,* John thought. Trade ships never came that far. Certainly not so late in the season.

After a couple more days, John insisted, "Let's go. Any trade ship passing here would be too far offshore to stop anyway."

"Just a little farther along the beach," Peter urged.

"Come on. We lit the signal fire. If anyone wants to stop, they'll stop."

Peter knew John was right. But then . . . on the horizon. . . .

"Look!" Peter grabbed John's arm and pointed out to sea. John shaded his eyes and squinted hard. Sure enough, it was a ship!

"Too far away," John said. "I don't think they can see the signal—" But then, "No, wait! Is she dropping anchor?"

Indeed, already a little past and with fair wind in her sails, the *Greyhound* did nevertheless come to anchor. Peter rowed out, and as he climbed aboard, Captain Anthony Gother reached down to give him a hand.

"I say!" said Captain Gother. "You ever hear of a lad name of John Newton? I have an important message for him."

# CHAPTER 13

# 1747

*"I was no further changed than a tiger tamed by hunger.
Remove the occasion, and he will be as wild as ever."*

"I CAN'T BELIEVE MY FATHER ACTUALLY GOT MY LETTERS!" JOHN exclaimed to Captain Gother who had insisted on accompanying Peter back to shore.

"For a year and a half I have searched," the captain replied. "I traced you to Mr. Clow, but when he told me you had moved far away, I abandoned my quest. But now we can head for England. Come, we must leave immediately before the tides turn."

To Captain Gother's surprise, John didn't answer.

"What's wrong with you?" Peter said. "Go!"

"Things have changed," John said slowly. "When I wrote to my father, I was miserable. But now I'm doing extremely well. I like living in Africa." He fingers closed around the goat skin bag hanging from his neck.

Captain Gother looked on, helpless and confused. He stood to collect a large reward if he brought John home. But after coming this close, were he to fail. . . .

"Surely you want to see the packet of letters I have for you," the captain said. "And there is the matter of the inheritance. Four hundred pounds a year, I believe."

"Inheritance?" John asked. "Who died?"

"I don't know the details, only that you stand to live a very comfortable life. But of course you have to come back to England to claim it."

"Well . . ." John said, hesitating. "There is Mary. . . ."

In the end, it was the hope of seeing Mary again that convinced John to leave. Only after the *Greyhound* was under full sail, and Kittam had faded into the distance, did Captain Gother admit to making up the story about the inheritance. "Now, now, it was for your own good," he hastened to say. "You are an Englishman, after all, and it's high time you got back to your own country." He quickly added, "I don't expect any work from you, of course. You're my guest. . . ." But John didn't calm down until Captain Gother said, "I do have letters for you," and handed over a stack, with ones from Mary on top.

All in all, it wasn't a bad deal: Lodging in the captain's cabin . . . dining at his table . . . no work required . . . just bide his time until he got back to England and Mary. But as the weeks dragged into months, John grew increasingly restless. One day, his irritation palpable, he gazed out to sea starboard, then crossed the deck and gazed out port side. Something wasn't right. "Mallory!" John called. "Where are we?"

"Cape Lopez," First Mate Mallory said.

"What?!" John exclaimed. "That's a thousand miles farther from home! It's been five months. We could have loaded up with Africans and been half way to England!"

"Takes a lot longer to accumulate a cargo hold of gold, ivory, dyers' wood, and beeswax," Mallory said.

"Well, I'm *#%! tired of sitting on my *&# in the #&*!* sun waiting to get home!" John stormed.

The first mate stopped, his eyebrows raised. "Well, well. I do think we're beginning to see a different side of John Newton."

Another year of waiting. The deal was that John wouldn't have to work, but illness and death reduced the crew from twenty to twelve, leaving the ship seriously undermanned. Aware of John's experience, Captain Gother assumed that under the circumstances he would help out. Wrong. Although the overworked crew had been slashed almost in half, John refused to lift a hand. When anyone dared suggest otherwise, he responded rudely. To pass the time, John amused himself with mathematics. When even that grew old, he took up a Bible and searched it for things to ridicule.

"Stop it!" the captain warned, even though he was quick to spout his own share of swear words. "I won't have blasphemy on my ship!"

"What do you have in mind?" John mocked. "Throwing me overboard? Maybe I'd just walk back to the ship across the water!"

With nothing but time on his hands, John found plenty of ways to make mischief. Once again, he managed to get his hands on a keg of rum, which immediately attracted a group of sailors around him. "My years in Africa weren't wasted," he proclaimed in a loud voice. "I learned to cast spells. For my first miracle, I will turn this rum into wine!" Folding his hands, he rolled his eyes upward as though deep in prayer. The sailors, imbibing freely, laughed uproariously.

Captain Gother strode over, barely able to contain his rage. "Stop that right now!" he ordered.

"Why, Captain," John said. "I never took you for an overly religious man."

"I may not be overly religious, but I know when to keep my mouth shut and my eye on heaven. I suggest you do the same."

Smirking, John took a noisy swig of rum. Then, holding the bottle out to the captain, he said, "Holy water, Sir?"

Had John been a crewman, Captain Gother could have punished him for profanity and blasphemy—quite severely, in fact. But John wasn't a crewman. He was a passenger. And the captain could do nothing to a passenger.

How John reveled in his power! Day after day, he invented new profanities that the rest of the crew quickly seized and mimicked. He knew exactly how to keep the sailors loyal to him, too. All he had to do was provide them with drink. John himself wasn't a good drinker, and normally he knew better than to test his limit. Still, one night out behind the mizzenmast, he showed up with an armload of bottles and a large sea shell, and challenged everyone within earshot to a drinking game. First a round of Dutch gin, then a round of rum. As the seashell passed from one to another, round after round, the men grew the worse for drink. Of all, however, John was worst off. Suddenly he jumped up and started dancing around the deck like a madman.

"Look at him go!" one sailor slurred.

"Stupid fool," said another.

Suddenly a gust of wind caught his hat and blew it over the side of the ship.

"My #$@* hat!" John spouted as he ran to peer over the side. By the light of the moon, he spied the longboat tied below. "I'll go get it in the boat!"

Had he not been so drunk, he would have realized he couldn't possibly jump all the way to the boat. But his judgment long gone, John scrambled up the railing and plunged over the side.

The sailors stared. Finally one took off his hat and said, "John can't swim."

The others did the same. "Poor John," they intoned. Had they not been so drunk themselves, someone might have attempted a rescue. Or at least a call for help.

THUMP! . . . THUMP! . . . THUMP! . . . So loud was the

noise from below that the watch officer came running to see what had happened. When the others stammered out that John Newton jumped overboard, he ran to the side and peered into the ocean.

"What the . . . ?" The watch officer grabbed a rope and threw it over. "John's jacket is snagged!" he said. "He's hanging on the side!" After hauling John up—completely dry and none the worse for his ordeal except that he was missing his jacket—the officer shook his head and said, "Someone up above is watching over you . . . although for the life of me I can't understand why."

As Captain Gother and his first mate sat together over dinner the next evening, Mallory asked, "Where's Newton?"

"I don't know," the captain said. "But I'll tell you, I regret ever laying eyes on him. He's the most profane troublemaker I ever did encounter."

"He is that," Mallory agreed.

"And it worries me. So many things going wrong on this voyage. That mast snapping the other day. And the surgeon taking sick, then dying before morning—"

"You saying it's somehow Newton's fault?"

"I'm saying at best he's a bad influence on the men. At worst he's a curse."

By January, nine months after John boarded the *Greyhound*, almost everyone on the ship despised him. Even the most hardened seamen were sick to death of his outrageous conduct and foul language. The disgusting tales he contrived by twisting Bible stories, the way he corrupted and ridiculed the words of Jesus—it left everyone disgusted and frightened. And seven thousand miles still lay between them and England.

Alone and bored, John picked up Thomas a' Kempis's book *The Imitation of Christ*. A most unlikely choice, as it explored the teachings of Jesus. John thought it might be good for a laugh. Or perhaps he would find something new to ridicule. What he read, however, made him extremely uncomfortable: God's judgment and punishment for sins. All he could think was, *What if these things are true?* Finally, unable to stand it any longer, he slammed the book shut. *True or false,* he thought, *I must abide by the consequences of my own choice.*

✦

Steaming with fury, Captain Gother stood in the doorway of his cabin watching John's latest antics. As thunder roared and lightening flashed, John dashed back and forth across the deck calling, "I'm over here! Now I'm over here! What's the matter, God? Your aim off? Can't seem to get me? Not good for someone supposed to be infallible!"

A few sailors dared snicker, but most quailed at such an audacious display.

"John!" Captain Gother ordered. "That's enough!"

"Why?" John shot back. "God hasn't got me yet!"

"Stop it this minute!" the captain roared. He strode over and grabbed John by the arm, yanking him off his feet. John stumbled to the deck. "You know the Scriptures," Gother said. "With my own eyes I have seen you read *Imitations of Christ.* Yet you behave like this. Do you fear nothing? May God have mercy on us all!"

By March, the *Greyhound* had made Newfoundland. As a diversion for the bored and weary crew, Captain Gother ordered a break to allow everyone time to fish. It seemed to work, for everyone was in an uncommonly good mood.

"I suppose we'll smoke the cod they catch, although heaven knows we don't need it," Gother told Mallory. "We have plenty of provisions to last the rest of our trip."

"Sir," Mallory began hesitantly, "if you will allow me to say so, after two years in the tropics, this ship is in rather poor condition. Do you think it can stand up to the stormy weather we're likely to encounter on the way home?"

Time and warm waters had indeed played havoc. Again and again the crew had caulked over the ship's shrunken, splitting timbers. The bottom of the hull was infested with worms. Patched sails had been taken down so the patches could be darned. Even the cordage showed signs of serious wear.

Looking to the sky, Captain Gother sighed. "It would take a good deal of time to boil up pitch and fill the holes. And as for the other repairs . . . We have a hard westerly wind. If it continues, it will push us fast to England."

"Let's pray that it does," said Mallory.

"Hoist the anchors!" Captain Gother ordered. "We're headed home."

## CHAPTER 14

# 1748

*"The coast of Guinea is a country from which few travelers, who have once ventured to settle there, ever return. But God, against whom I had sinned with a high hand, was pleased to appoint me to be a singular instance of his mercy. When I seemed bent upon my own destruction, he provided for my deliverance."*

JOHN AWAKENED TO THE CRASH OF SPLINTERING TIMBERS. AS THE SHIP tossed violently, icy salt water suddenly poured down on him from the deck above. Leaping from his soaked bunk, John splashed into half a foot of water.

"All hands on deck!" First Mate Mallory bellowed. "The ship is sinking!"

John dashed from his cabin and started up the ladder, but Captain Gother pulled him back. "Go get your knife!" he ordered. When John ran back with his knife, a burly sailor pushed him aside and ran up the ladder ahead of him. But as the sailor stepped onto the deck, an enormous wave swept across, washing him overboard.

"All hands on deck! All hands on deck!"

Already the wildly tossing sea had torn away the ship's upper timbers port side. Everywhere planks, wrenched loose, drooped and dangled. The ship was a wreck. Men grabbed up pots, pails, anything they could use to bail water. A bucket floated by. Snatching it up, John set to work.

"Lash ye'selfs to the closest thing wot can't move, mateys!" a sailor named Reggie shouted. Even as he spoke, a rolling wave swept away the sailor next to John.

In the chaos, barrel after barrel of provisions washed overboard. Crates of live animals tumbled across the deck, then they too went over. With the halyards snapped, the sails couldn't be lowered, and the wind whipped them to shreds. As the last tatters of the topsails blew away, another wave hit, cracking the main mast down the middle.

"Hard to starboard!" Captain Gother commanded in a hoarse voice. The pilot strained to turn the wheel and meet an oncoming surge head on.

"I can't believe the ship hasn't sunk!" John gasped.

"It's the cargo wot does it," Reggie told him. "Beeswax and wood is lighter'n water. They keeps her afloat."

Falling timbers battered the deck. Without warning, Reggie shoved John, sending him sprawling. John jumped up, fists clenched, yelling, "You #*%!" A heavy rigging pulley plunged from the mast above and crashed to the deck right on the spot John had stood seconds before, crushing Reggie.

John gaped in horror. Then he dropped to his knees on the flooded deck. Lifting his face to heaven, he cried, "Father! Help me! The ship is sinking, and I can't swim!"

Hour after hour, with almost every wave breaking high over their heads, the men fought gallantly to keep the ship afloat. After two years in a hot climate, the icy waters and freezing wind compounded their bone-crushing weariness. Misery on top of despair. "If this will not do," John said, "then God have mercy on us!" The minute the words left of his mouth, it struck him: *What mercy can there be for me?*

At three the next morning, John made his way below deck to work the bilge pumps, and there he stayed until noon. Every time the ship plunged down into the sea, he fully expected it to sink to the bottom. And for the first time in years, he dreaded death.

After manning the pumps for nine straight hours, John, on the verge of collapse, dragged himself to his bunk and fell into a deep sleep. But barely an hour later he was summoned to the helm. For the next eleven hours, he steered the ship through the heaving sea. Mountainous swells smashed against the badly listing wreck, threatening to overturn it. This time, instead of boasting about being the captain of his own soul, he spent the time contemplating his life. *Never was there such a sinner as I*, he thought with despair. *Surely my sins are too great to be forgiven. If this ship goes down, I will go to hell!* Willingly he had turned his back on God. If God was fair, John would not survive.

*If only it were true that Jesus Christ was God's Son who died so that my great sins could be forgiven!* John thought. Long-forgotten verses popped into his mind: "I will mock when your fear cometh . . ." and "Then shall they call upon me but I will not hear." Sadly resigned, John waited for the end. Then, another verse from his childhood came to him. It was Luke 6:13: "If ye, being evil, know how to give good gifts to your children, how much more shall your heavenly Father give the Holy Spirit to them that ask him?"

At six o'clock that evening—after five hours at the helm—John bowed his head and he asked. Immediately the sea began to calm.

In the last shadows before twilight, shivering men huddled on the deck in water up to their ankles, gazing around them at their disaster of a ship. The *Greyhound* was a floating ruin. The few wooden casks of provisions that hadn't washed overboard lay where they were beaten to pieces by the waves. Pigs and goats and sheep and chickens—all washed overboard. Of the ample store of food, only the cod they caught in Newfoundland and fresh water survived. Wind rustled through the scraps of sails clinging to the broken masts, and the hull gaped with holes.

As the shrunken timbers swelled, leaks popped before their eyes. Already Geoffrey Alexander, the ship's carpenter, frantically stuffed bedding into the worst of the holes and nailed boards to hold the stuffing in place. "More blankets, Mates!" he ordered. "Get me pillows . . . anything!" Then he said, "Take off your clothes, and I'll use them, too!" He pulled off his own wet trousers and shirt, and stuffed them into a hole.

The sailors stared numbly until the captain barked, "That's an order! Strip!" He tugged off his own clothes and offered them to Alexander, who quickly plugged them into a leak. John stepped up and did the same. Then, one by one, the others followed.

The next day dawned bright and calm, yet the surviving men shivered in the cold northern air. Captain Gother, himself almost bare, didn't bother to call them to attention. "I wish I could tell you our ordeal is over," he said solemnly. "Unfortunately, it's just beginning. As you can see, the ship is badly damaged. We will need to pump around the clock. Our provisions are almost gone, and the sails all but useless. I strongly suggest everyone pray, for only by God's grace will we live to see home." Casting a scathing look at John, he added, "If we do, it will be no thanks to the accursed Jonah on board."

Even if they'd had food, the galley was washed away. And the only firewood left was soaking wet. Besides the case of dried cod, all they found was a barrel of pig food. Barely enough to last them a week.

By day, a human chain of pathetic men passed buckets and

pots and pans of water up the ladder, across the deck, and over the side of the ship in a desperate attempt to drain the ship's hold. Those who could be spared pulled down the shredded sails and did their best to stitch the pieces together. Under Alexander's direction, others wound thick ropes around the cracked main mast to try to keep it from splitting completely in two. Each night the men sank down onto the hard floor, and, without clothes or bedding, shivered themselves into an exhausted sleep. But after only a couple of hours they were awakened to once again bail water.

"We can't work no more! Not with no rest!" one sailor complained to Mallory. To which Mallory snapped, "Would you rather rest forever at the bottom of the sea?"

Shivering on his bunk, John remembered his long ago dream about the ring. Could it be that this was the very event foretold? Perhaps his prayer as he stood at the helm was him asking for the ring back. "I must make certain I'm worthy of another chance," he breathed.

"Hoist the sails," Captain Gother called after Alexander attached two tiny stitched-together replacements to the halyards. With the hoisting, a hopeful cheer went up from the beleaguered crew. Those makeshift sails proved to be surprisingly adequate, especially considering what the men had to work with. Smiling broadly, John turned to find himself facing the captain. He was not smiling.

"This is the greatest disaster of my life, Newton!" he said. "I rue the day I ever laid eyes on you. Most of my cargo is gone, the ship is in ruins, and good seamen lay at the bottom of the sea. I told you your actions would bring down God's punishment. Would that I had cast you overboard the first time you dared blaspheme his name!"

"It was a storm, Captain—" John began, but Gother cut him off.

"Don't you tell me!" he hissed. "I've been in plenty of storms in my time, and this was no ordinary storm. Punishment by God, it was! I've half a mind to throw you over right now. Maybe it still isn't too late to set things to right."

"Captain, I should tell you—"

"No, *I* should tell *you*! You stay out of my way, if you value your life!"

As the *Greyhound* sailed slowly and unevenly, sailors sprawled on the sun-washed deck. "No food," one said. "No wind in the sails. And precious little 'twixt us and our mates wot sleeps in the deep."

"The devil's laying fer the lot of us," another said.

Yet not a curse word came from John's mouth. Not one blasphemous joke crossed his lips. Instead of joining the men on deck, or climbing up to sit beside those lining the bare yards or hanging in the shrouds watching for land, John spent his free time reading the Bible and praying for mercy. He had to admit that he could not say from his heart he believed the gospel. Still, he clung to it and continued studying.

Though the wind blew fair, the listing ship made little progress. The sailors—weary to death of standing endlessly in cold water working the flooded pumps—plunged into despair. The fact was, with all their navigational tools destroyed, none of them really knew where they were. About a hundred leagues from shore, they guessed. (Actually, they were much farther out than that.)

✦

About a week after the storm, John was awakened one morning by shouts from the deck watch: "Land ho! Land ho! I see land! We're saved!"

And an uncommonly beautiful dawn it was, too. Straight ahead, about twenty miles out, stood a mountainous coast. And a bit beyond that, several small islands stuck up out of the water.

"The northwest tip of Ireland!" the watch called triumphantly.

Yes! Their goal exactly. If the wind held, just one more day and they would safely put their feet on land. And sit down to a real meal with food! Within minutes, the deck overflowed with excited men, laughing and talking and cheering Captain Gother who carefully surveyed the area with his spyglass.

"I see it!" the captain announced. "Three small islands rising out of the water."

The men went wild with excitement.

"Break out the two pints of brandy we have left, Mr. Mallory," Captain Gother said. "Divide up the last of the bread, too. We are going to celebrate!"

Below decks rocked with joyous noise as the men savored their precious allotment of brandy and bread. What a lovely accompaniment to dried cod! It was the last of their food, but what did that matter? By tomorrow their plates would overflow.

"A toast to dry ground!" a sailor called out, and all the others lifted their mugs and cried, "Hear, hear! To dry ground!"

Then a somber Captain Gother stepped through the doorway and everyone fell silent. "It won't be dry land today," he said. "Nor tomorrow nor the next day either."

"What?" John asked in confusion. "But the islands—"

"No islands," Gother said. "Just clouds. It was all a mirage."

Within half an hour, the horizon showed nothing but an endless expanse of sea. As the "mountains" dissolved, so did the sailors' last hope, for they had just gobbled up everything but the dregs of cod in the corners of the fish barrel. Where the deck had so recently rung with cheers, it now resounded with curses—from everyone except John.

"The wind still blows fair," John said.

"It does," Captain Gother agreed. "If it continues, we will surely hit land soon."

But that day the wind stopped. By the next, the sea lay before them oily calm.

"It couldn't be worse!" Mallory mourned.

Actually, it could. The next morning, a gale blew from southwest, driving them away from Ireland and toward Scotland, beyond any hope of rescue. No ships sailed that part of the ocean at that time of year. Absolutely none—except for one decrepit wreck.

Each day the surviving men sat down, shivering and their lips blue with cold, to divide up the day's allotment of one half a cod. Then it was back to work at the pumps. They didn't dare let up for a moment or the struggling ship would sink. And the wind, capricious and fickle, alternately threatened to leave them stranded to starve to death, or to toss the broken ship over and drown them all. On windless days, the two small patched sails hung lifelessly, hardly casting a shadow across the glassy ocean as the sun quickly grew maliciously hot. If they weren't freezing, they were burning.

After another two weeks, despondency settled over the crew. One afternoon Captain Gother spotted three men sprawled on the deck. "What's the matter with you?" he exclaimed. "Why are you lying here in the sun?"

"Cain't pump no more," said Ned. "We's too weak from starvin'."

"Well, get yourselves below and out of the hot sun," the captain said.

"Too tired to climb down the ladder," Davis mumbled.

"I just dropped one dead man overboard," Captain Gother snapped. "I don't plan on losing another today. Now get below! That's an order."

Not one of the sailors moved. "We's all dead men," Davis said. "Don't do you no good to give orders to the dead."

Captain Gother simply turned and walked away.

"It was Billy what died," Ned told the others. "If cap'n didn't throw him over, we could'a eat tonight."

"Not me!" Davis replied. "Unh, uh! I'm no cannibal!"

"I'm not talking about killing no one. Jist using the ones who is already dead. I think it makes a whole lot of sense," said Ned.

"Sure do to me," rumbled the other man. "Surely do. Next mate who dies. . . ."

✦

John, still wet from working the pumps, was at his desk reading the Bible when Captain Gother burst in with Mallory right behind. "Just when I think our plight can't get any worse, it does," he growled. "We have no fresh water. Those four kegs we were depending on are all empty. Punctured during the storm."

"Captain," John began, "I know you consider me part of the cause of this—"

"Part of the cause?" Gother bellowed. "I consider you the sole cause! You think you're helping us sitting here reading that Bible? It's too late for that. You're the Jonah who caused this, and I want you off my ship . . . now!"

"You're throwing me overboard?"

"Aye," Captain Gother said. "I should have done it long ago and saved all of us this calamity." He motioned to Mallory, who stepped forward and bound John's wrists. "My only regret is having to face your father—though I doubt I'll live to worry about it."

"Captain, this is murder!" John protested.

"Save your defense for the Almighty God."

John struggled to climb the ladder with his hands tied. But no sooner had he emerged on the main deck than a gentle wind blew into their faces. The captain and Mallory looked up at the makeshift sails. Sure enough, they were filling. Not a strong wind, which would have quickly blown the patched sails apart. Just a perfect wind.

"Cut him loose," Captain Gother told Mallory.

As the ship limped forward, the watch called, "Land ho! Land ho!"

On April 8,1748—three full months after the storm—the *Greyhound* dropped anchor off the shore of Lough Swilly, Ireland. With their last bit of strength, nine scraggly survivors managed a cheer. When the good people of Lough Swilly caught sight of the pitiful wreck, they immediately rowed out in longboats to fetch the survivors. As they rowed toward shore, the wind whipping up again, John turned and looked just as the *Greyhound* rolled over on her side. "There is a God in heaven," John gasped, "and he does hear and answer prayer!"

# CHAPTER 15

# 1748

*"I was no longer an infidel. I was touched with a sense of God's undeserved mercy. Although I consider this the beginning of my return to God, I cannot consider myself to have been a believer in the full sense of the word until much later."*

As THE IRISH TOWNSFOLK OPENED THEIR HOMES TO THE DESPERATE survivors, filling their empty stomachs with boiled lamb and potatoes and fresh baked bread and swaddling them in warm blankets, the wind once again roared out its violence. Shuddering, John pulled closer to the roaring fire. One more night on that shattered ship and every one of them would have gone down into the icy sea.

"We went to the gates of hell," Captain Gother said, and no one disagreed.

From that day forward, no curse word ever came from John Newton's mouth.

At sunrise next morning, Geoff Alexander directed the Irish carpenters, ". . . then swing the upper yards and spars aloft. Reseat them at the mastheads—once the mastheads are replaced. And the hull—" Here he simply shook his head and groaned.

While the ship underwent the long process of salvage and rebuilding, John made his way inland to Londonderry. So kindly was he received that several gentlemen invited him to join a shooting party with them and the mayor. Out in the countryside, John climbed a steep bank, pulling his shotgun after him. But the gun went off unexpectedly—so near his face it shot away the corner of his hat!

"Just when we think ourselves safe . . ." he wrote in a letter to his father that night.

Every day John grew stronger and healthier, and more determined to prove he truly was a different man. When he had tried to change before, he always focused on his sin. This time, he fixed his eyes on the undeserved mercy God extended to him. But he had no Christian friend to guide or encourage him. And although he went to church twice each day to pray, he had no opportunity to hear God's word preached. So while he acknowledged God's mercy in pardoning his wretched past, for the future, he continued to depend on his own resolutions to do better. And no one told him that wasn't enough.

Two years had passed since Captain Newton last heard from his son. Though it pained him terribly, he finally resigned himself to the facts that John's ship was lost at sea and his son was dead. In January, two months before the *Greyhound* limped into Lough Swilly, Captain Newton accepted a job as governor at the Hudson Bay Company's Fort York trading post in what is now Canada. Cold and hostile, Fort York was where Indian trappers came to trade fur pelts. It was also a point of defense for British interests against the French. Newton's minimum stay was to be three years. Just what Tomasin thought about this was never said. But she stayed in England with their now three children—besides William, twelve, and Henry, eight, there was little Thomasina, aged two.

Just days before he left London for Hudson's Bay, Captain Newton received John's letter from Londonderry. Sad timing. Newton desperately wanted John to come along with him and work as his personal assistant. He wanted to tell his son that all was forgiven. And John longed for his father to see how he had changed. If only they'd had time.

Several affectionate letters from his father awaited John, however. In one, Captain Newton said he had paid a visit to Kent. Since Mary was still single, he got George Catlett's consent for John to marry her. Then Newton added his own blessing.

"Hooray!" John whooped. Only one more consent to obtain—Mary's!

Unfortunately, John was in no financial condition to marry. If only he had gotten a salary on one of his voyages, and a share of the profits. With nowhere else to turn, he went to see Joseph Manesty. Manesty greeted him warmly and said, "My ship, the *Brownlow*, will be ready by summer. I was looking for a captain."

"Thank you," John said quickly, "but to tell the truth, Sir, I don't think I'm ready for such a position. It's true that I'm a skilled seaman, but I don't have as much experience in obedience and accepting responsibility."

"Well, now," Manesty said with a chuckle, "this *is* a new John Newton! And I must say, one that greatly impresses me. How about if you go on the *Brownlow* as first mate, and I reserve the position of captain for you on my next ship?"

Armed with this good news, John headed straight for Kent. Bluebells nodding along the roadside added to the joy in his heart. Tulips—red and pink and yellow—peeked from inside just about every gate. Aaahh, spring!

It was a different John Newton who greeted the Catletts and sat with them in their parlor that day. No more the strutting, immature braggart. "Everything is different now," he said, struggling for words. "I . . . I don't know how to explain it to you."

After John told his story, Mrs. Catlett exclaimed through her tears, "Oh, John! Your mother would be so pleased!"

After a moment of awkwardness, John asked, "Mary, will you walk with me?"

As soon as Mary agreed, little Sara squealed, "Me too! I'll go!" But Mrs. Catlett put out her hand and shook her head, hushing the little girl.

The woods were beautiful, with all the trees in bloom. For awhile, John and Mary walked in silence. Then John said, "I have loved you since the day I first saw you. I would be a good husband to you, that I promise."

"We don't know each other that well," Mary said. "And, really, I'm not ready to marry anyone just yet."

Struggling to hide his disappointment, John asked, "Maybe after I get back from my next voyage? Mr. Manesty has a ship for me. When the slaves are sold, I'm sure to come back with a good profit."

Mary thought for a moment, then she said, "Some say the Africans are treated horribly on those ships."

"We teach them to be civilized," John said, "and give them a chance for heaven."

"Hmmm," Mary mused. "Most who are against the slave trade are Christians."

"I happen to know that Mr. Manesty owns half a pew at St. George's Church in Liverpool. Slavery is a legal and honorable business, Mary."

"I suppose you're right," Mary said with a sigh. "You are a wise person."

In July 1748, at the age of twenty-three, John once again sailed for Africa. In addition to the usual store of provisions, the

*Brownlow*'s captain laid in a supply of branding irons, yokes, chains, and iron shackles.

"Food?" John asked Captain Robert Jackson, pointing to the sacks of dried grain.

"Not for us," the captain replied with a laugh. "Mix it with water and it makes excellent gruel for the slaves. They will eat it all the way across the Atlantic."

Captain Jackson was overjoyed to discover that his first mate had experience with traders on the African coast. He was well aware that they were flush with wealth and power, and that they lived extravagantly. And that in order to get the best slaves, a ship's captain must indulge them. But just how to go about it, he wasn't at all certain.

"We can't do business without good contacts," Captain Jackson said to John. "I trust yours are dependable. . . ."

Many a captain who tried to take advantage of African traders—or was suspected of it—ended up with his boat attacked, or set adrift, or even set on fire. So Captain Jackson, ever cautious, decided John should be the one to sail from place to place in the longboat and do the purchasing. A plan that didn't displease John, by the way. He quite relished the idea of being the one to demonstrate the right way to do things. Sort of an opportunity to let everyone know who was boss. So, accompanied by three seamen and an officer by the name of Oliver Blue, John made his way upriver. As the others rowed, he guided them to the slave compound.

Ignoring the misery around him, John strode up and down between the manacled captives. He had no intention of being taken for a fool by the experienced slave dealers. The old . . . the small . . . the lame or defective—those, he immediately rejected. Carefully he checked each man and woman for rotten teeth, for disease, for even the slightest malformation.

"We can get lesser ones for a better price," Oliver reasoned. "Why go for the best? What does it matter to us?"

"It matters a great deal," John said. "Unless they are extremely healthy, they won't survive the voyage. We can't sell them in the slave markets unless they're alive and ready to work and breed for their new masters."

At night, John joined the African traders around the fire. Lying back, he traced the constellations that glowed brilliantly in the ebony sky. How he enjoyed the familiar sounds of the jungle after dark! And the old smells of excitement and possibility.

From the men's section, John chose several strong young men. In the women's area, he took a shy young woman who shrank back from his touch. Then he inspected a girl of about twelve, and, smiling appreciatively, he picked her. Also a young mother. . . . "But not the baby," he instructed as he turned away. Immediately an overseer snatched the infant from the horrified mother. John could hear her screaming.

"Nothing here that interests us," John said as they passed the children's section. But a young boy, staring straight ahead with no emotion, caught his eye. "That one," John said pointing him out to Oliver Blue. "How old do you think he is?"

Oliver shrugged. "Ten? Maybe eleven?"

"Pretty brave for an eleven-year-old," John mused. Then to the trader, "I'll take him." But when the overseers tried to separate him from the smaller boy next to him, the older boy growled and fought and clung to the little one. "Brothers," John said with a sigh. "Well, give me both of them."

After John made his choices, his shipmates bound the captives' wrists, then attached them all together by rope and marched them to the longboat. John stayed behind to settle the bill.

"Sixty bars per slave," the trader said.

This didn't refer to actual bars of gold or silver, but to an agreed upon amount of trade goods. Supply and demand determined the price. John paid with two crates of rifles and several bolts of cotton cloth.

As John headed toward the boat, a man on the path ahead picked up a stick and thrashed the slave he had just purchased until the poor African slumped to the ground and lay still. Without breaking his stride, John stepped on the man's back and kept walking.

✦

"Excellent choices!" Captain Jackson exclaimed as he surveyed the new purchases. Then he commanded the sailors to "Pack them in. And be certain they are locked and bolted."

Rarely did Captain Jackson go ashore, except when he was required to meet with a tribal chief or join a trader for dinner. Pleased to have John take charge of purchasing the slaves, his compliments were lavish. Soon boasting crept back into John's conversation. Mockery followed, then ridicule. His carriage resumed its familiar arrogant stance, too. In fact, he was almost as bad as before—except no profanity and no blasphemy.

As the *Brownlow* wove along the river, through inlets and between clumps of trees, John carefully scanned the horizon. Then he spotted it, dead ahead: Clow's island. The seamen pulled the longboat up on shore and John stepped out onto the sand of the familiar cove. Two black slaves stopped work to stare. One whispered to the other, "It's John Newton, and what do you think? He has shoes on his feet!"

"Aye," said the other, "and stockings, too!" Never before had they seen him so.

"Bindo!" John called to the man who had saved his life. But the African just stared. "Bindo, it's me. John Newton!"

"John . . . Master . . . You come back!" Bindo looked uncertain, but John rushed over and hugged him. Bindo, stiff and uncomfortable, merely grunted.

"Tell Clow I'm here to collect the limes he owes me," John said.

Clow and Pae'ai greeted John as through he were a long lost friend: smiles, jokes, laughter, slaps on the back, a fine dinner served on fine china. Just as if nothing had ever happened between them. After dinner, Clow and Pae'ai invited John and his men to join them on the verandah for cool drinks. John was polite and businesslike, but he returned the smiles with cold indifference.

"Yessiree, John used to live here," Clow said to the others. "Helped me plant the lime groves. He tell you lads about that?"

"No, Sir," Oliver said. "He did trading with you?"

"That he did! I gave him his start."

"It was you who said I'd come back here one day on my own slave ship," John reminded him with a note of sarcasm. "Well, that's what I've done."

"That you did, my lad," Clow said with a hearty laugh. "Ain't that something? I predicted it, and that's just what you did!"

Then Clow called out to Pae'ai, "Woman! Get our guests something more to eat and drink. Can't let honored guests go wanting!"

John's men spent the night in Clow's lodging, but John slept in his old house . . . until he awakened in the early hours of the morning drenched in sweat. When he tried to stand up, he fell back to his mat, clenching his throbbing head. "Oh, no!" he prayed. "Please, dear God, not again! Not here!"

He managed to make his way to the door, then down to

the water's edge before slumping into the sand. "Please, God, please . . . Give me another chance," he prayed. "Spare my life one more time!" No resolves. No deals. No promises. For once in his life, John simply threw himself on God's mercy. "Forgive me. Do what is best in your sight." And in the cave where he once sought shelter from Clow, he collapsed and lay unconscious as ocean wave after ocean wave washed over him.

When the moon was full in the sky, John got to his feet and lifted his face toward heaven. "My fever . . . it's gone!" he exclaimed. "Thank you, God! Thank you!" Two days later, a completely healthy John Newton sailed from Clow's island.

✦

"Pack the slaves in tight," Oliver Blue ordered the crew down in the deck below. "Captain's orders. He wants a full load."

"Eight months' work," John said. "One more stop, and we can set sail."

"But, Sir." Oliver said, "John. . . . We're already at capacity."

"Captain says we need a few more males," John said.

"But they're already two deep down there," Oliver protested. "As you yourself said, they aren't worth anything if they don't survive."

John stepped down and surveyed the hold. Sure enough, chained slaves filled every inch of space.

"Not another place to lay a body or an extra chain to lock them up," Oliver said.

"You will have to make room," John replied as he disappeared through the hatch.

Oliver Blue picked his way over to the two boys—the brave eleven-year-old and his little brother. First he tossed the little one overboard, then the older one. A woman went next, then another woman who screamed and fought to the end.

Before leaving Africa, John took his place in the longboat with several others, ready to gather wood and water for the return trip. Suddenly Captain Jackson called, "John! Back on the ship! Bates, you take his place." Confused, John asked why the change. Jackson just shrugged and said, "I don't know. I just decided you should stay on board today." At nightfall, word came that the longboat had sunk and all hands drowned. Slowly Captain Jackson turned and stared at John. "Well," he said. "The good Lord must have some important plan for you."

Packed full with 218 slaves, the *Brownlow* set sail for the island of Antigua. This journey across the Atlantic from Africa to the rich slave markets of the New World, known as the Middle Passage, was the most dangerous of the triangular routes. For the poor Africans chained on their sides, "spoon-packed" with not an inch between them, it was a trip fraught with agony and great danger. So stifling was the airless hold that candles wouldn't even burn. Night and day, screams and groans echoed through the ship. It almost drove John to distraction. "Can't you shut them up?" he demanded of Oliver.

Every day, sailors lugged a huge pot of gruel down the ladder to the hold where they slapped a ladleful into the outstretched hand of each slave. Anyone too weak to reach out got nothing. And when any died, the bodies lay chained to their companions until someone found it convenient to unlock them and throw them overboard, along with any others deemed too sick to survive. May as well save an extra trip down.

"Ugh," John groaned when he passed by the open hatch to the ship's hold. "What a revolting stench! They have to be the most unclean creatures that ever lived."

"We're getting ready to clean them up," Captain Jackson said. "Now that they're thinning out, it will be easier."

Hobbled with leg chains and weakened from their excruciatingly cramped quarters, the captives struggled up the stairs and huddled together on the deck. One young woman hugged a newborn baby to her chest. At the captain's command, Oliver pulled the infant from her arms and tossed it overboard. Even John gasped.

"She can't care for it," Captain Jackson explained. "Better a quick drowning than slow starvation. I'm not heartless, John." Then he ordered, "The lash, Mr. Blue."

Two seamen began beating a rhythm on the drums. Crudely calling out a few words in an African tongue, Oliver grabbed up a whip and lashed at the huddled slaves. Stiffly at first, then more and more wildly, they danced as best they could with their ankles in chains. The assembled crew laughed and clapped, and hooted and cheered.

"Keeps them fit and healthy," Captain Jackson called out to John. But from the looks on the men's faces, entertainment was the more likely goal. A reward for mucking out the filthy hold. When the dancing ended, the crew threw buckets of sea water on the slaves to clean them up. Then, soaking wet, they were herded back to their prison. "Tonight," the captain announced cheerily, "you may each have your pick of a slave girl. You earned it." The men cheered and stomped their feet.

"That cute little one," Oliver said to John with a wink and a grin, "we've saved her just for you."

Women. John's constant temptation.

It was on the *Brownlow* that John got his first taste of the slavers' greatest dread—slave rebellion. Before order was restored, four Africans and one seaman lay dead. Also during the trip, John helped bury seven sailors who perished with the fever.

When Antigua came into view, the surviving slaves were brought up on deck and released from their leg irons and manacles. Freedom! What joy! Hosed down, scrubbed clean, and shaved, they were polished with olive oil and beeswax until their skin shone like silk. Laughing and chattering, they had no idea that the worst was yet to come. Then he said, "Load them back in. Prices are too low. We'll sail on to Charleston."

By the time the *Brownlow* reached America, sixty slaves had died—more than a quarter of those who left Africa. Rewashed and re-oiled for display, John and Oliver herded the slaves to an open air exchange behind the post office, just a short walk from the wharf. With an expert hand, Oliver quickly culled out the "refuse slaves," those too ill to generate any interest on the auction block, and dumped them quayside to join the unwanted from other ships. Most likely, they would starve to death.

At the auction block, husbands were ripped from wives, parents from children, brother from sister. After already losing so much, they must part again—most likely forever. John watched, unmoved. Even on the days he wrote to Mary of his undying love for her. Even on the day he asked her to be his wife. One more paradox of his life.

Almost every day, John wandered to the woods and fields to pray. Yet he came back to spend his evenings in taverns with his shipmates, where he laughed and cheered on their loud, boisterous behavior. While he never missed Sunday service, and he soaked in everything he heard from the pulpit, once outside the church, he treaded on the brink of sin, always ready to flirt with temptation.

It took six weeks in Charleston, South Carolina, to sell the slaves and clean up the ship, then to reload the hull with cotton and tobacco. Six weeks before the *Brownlow* was ready to set sail for home.

CHAPTER 16

# 1750

*"The necessity of another absence seemed to me as bitter as death. But God had other lessons for me to learn."*

"THANK YOU, SIR!" JOHN SAID AS HE SHOOK JOSEPH MANESTY'S HAND and pocketed his pay plus his share of the ship's profits. Not riches, to be sure, but enough money to allow him to hold his head up in front of the Catletts and assure them of his financial security.

"Next ship out, you'll be Captain John Newton!" Manesty promised.

Life was good! Money in his pocket and respect from his employer, permission to marry his love with his father's blessing, and Mary's acceptance of his proposal. Seven long years, but his dearest dream was about to finally become reality.

On February 12, 1750, twenty-five-year-old John Newton married Mary Catlett, twenty-one, at St. Margaret's Church in Chatham, England. From that day forward, John hardly ever spoke her name. To him, she was always "my dearest." Throughout the spring, the newlyweds strolled together for hours on end. A countryside in bloom, gardens awakening in glorious color, and a future of happiness to discuss together. Almost more joy than John could contain.

As spring moved into summer, however, John nervously counted his dwindling savings. Money was going fast. With the end of summer would come shipping season, but how could he leave his new wife? In desperation, John bought a handful of lottery tickets hoping one would make him rich. Instead, his wild purchase plunged him into debt to the tune of seventy pounds. And so, with the waning of summer, John roused himself from his glorious three-month dream and contacted Joseph Manesty.

"I was getting ready to send a messenger for you," Manesty responded. "I've refitted the *Duke of Argyle* and she's ready to go."

What torture for John to tear himself away from his dearest! And yet, as he neared the docks, his thoughts returned to the sea. Despite all, when it came time to raise the anchor, his heart leapt with eager anticipation.

The *Duke of Argyle* was not what John had envisioned. To be exact, it verged on decrepit. Not much better than the *Greyhound* after two full years at sea.

"Captain Newton!" Joseph Manesty called out in greeting. "Welcome! Your ship awaits you."

Captain Newton. Yes, he truly was the captain! Who could blame him for swelling a bit with pride? And for overlooking the ship's weaknesses? Manesty introduced him to his first mate, Simon Andrews, then to the other officers. "We put in an extra shelf for tight pack," said Jason Cunningham, the ship's carpenter.

On August 13, 1750, Captain John Newton gave the command to weigh anchor and set the sails for Africa. Once under way, he assembled the entire crew of thirty men and laid out his rules. "Rules make a ship run smoothly," he stated. His included a ceremonial send-off anytime the ship was docked and he should leave. In addition, the crew must keep a close look-out, because as soon as he returned they must give him a formal welcome. "It's only befitting a captain," he explained. "Oh, and about Sundays," he added, "the entire crew will gather on deck for worship at six bells in the forenoon. Then at seven bells in the afternoon, all will come together again for an evening Scripture lesson. I will lead both, and everyone's attendance is required. Also, first thing Sunday morning and immediately after dinner, all will meet for prayers. No exceptions."

If John noticed the grumbles and under-the-breath curses, he didn't show it.

Every day, John wrote to Mary, even when he had no way to send her the letters. He simply held on to them until he arrived at a port, then he shipped the entire bundle. Amazingly, she received every single letter. Often he bragged about the men's affection for him. "Not a man on my ship will eat dinner until I give him leave," he wrote. "And if I stay out until midnight, no one presumes to shut their eyes until they have the honor of seeing me again."

How little he knew! In fact, the crew could barely disguise their resentment for his rules, and they detested his overbearing piety. He was his father all over again—only worse.

"Rumors of mutiny," Simon Andrews warned John more than once.

"Who is it this time?" John always demanded. "Give me names. They'll be in irons tonight and flogged tomorrow."

With the exception of the first and second mates—and Dr. Mann, the ship's surgeon—John declared the *Duke of Argyle* crew the worst bunch of scoundrels he ever had the misfortune to know. Crude . . . drunk . . . profane . . . forever inventing lewd songs and spouting foul language—in short, a lot like the old John Newton. Only now, those things sickened John. Of the lot, Will Lees was the worst.

"No!" Lees said one night when he was ordered to stand watch. "I will not."

"You will or your back will feel the lash," Andrews warned.

"That so? One scar across me back, and ye might not wake up next morning."

The threat worked. That night, Lees settled himself comfortably in his hammock, a satisfied smirk on his face, while Andrews pulled Ted Burke to stand watch. Still, John wrote to Mary, "I try to treat all of them with humanity. And I try to be a good example."

As soon as they anchored off the African coast, John ordered all hands on deck. "Whenever I'm not on board, Mr. Andrews will be here," he announced. "No one, not at any time or for any purpose, shall leave the ship without permission from one of us. That's an order!"

Will Lees dared to scowl openly, and several others joined him in protests. But John knew exactly how to placate his crew. "I'll bring women back with me," he promised. "Plenty for everyone." Whistles and laughter drowned out both Lees and the captain. When John finally restored order, he said, "Mr. Andrews will choose six of you to come with me in the longboat. We'll be back by evening with the first of the cargo."

Thus began seven months of trading up and down the coast. But with so much competition from so many slave ships, and with so many buyers intent on cheating the traders, the price of slaves soared to ninty bars each.

"Not a thing that can be adulterated is offered genuine!" John stormed to Andrews. "Watered-down rum. Gunpowder kegs fitted with false heads to make them look larger. So much cloth cut out of the middle of the bolts it's hard to see how it can be of any use at all. Well, it's robbery, and I won't be a part of it!"

As the hold filled with slaves, once again the background jungle hum was replaced with shrieks of agony and wailing. This time, however, John hardly seemed to notice. "Simon," he said cheerily to his first mate, "you ever sail on a merchant ship?"

"No," Andrews said. "But this is my fifth slaver."

"Well, there's a lot to be said for slavers. Easy compared to collecting for a merchant ship. That can take five years."

Andrews pondered a moment. Then he said, " 'Course gold and ivory and such don't rise up and chop you to bits in your sleep."

After seven months of making their way farther and farther upriver, sweltering in the heat and engulfed by clouds of ravenous mosquitoes, a crewman asked, "Why we fightin' our way so far inland?"

"Cargo is too picked over near the coast," John explained. "One more camp and we head for home." Later he confided to Andrews, "I have my eye on some good slaves tomorrow. Too many of ours are whip-marked. Troublemakers make me nervous."

Andrews, dripping with sweat, swatted lamely at the canopy of biting mosquitoes swarming around his head. "All I can say is, those Africans should fall down and thank the good Lord we're rescuing them from here."

That night, although Andrews had all but given up on him, Lees reported at midnight to stand the middle watch. But while the rest of the crew slept, he and Burke slipped over the side of the ship and into the longboat, then they rowed out to meet several men they had befriended from a French schooner moored nearby. And for the next several hours they drank down the rum the French sailors brought. Drunk and mean, Lees started a fight with the French—though he didn't fare nearly as well as he thought he would. When he and Burke tried to escape, they ran the longboat up onto rocks and couldn't pull it free. Next morning, when John and his party prepared to go ashore to make the final purchases, the longboat was gone. John watched helplessly as the captain of the French ship rowed ashore and bought the slaves John so desired.

When the troublemakers were delivered back to the ship, John pointed to Lees and bellowed, "Strip him and lay him across a barrel!" Grabbing up a cane, John whipped him mercilessly. "Clamp them both in irons," he ordered. "No, not below deck. Directly in the hot sun!"

"Hypocrite!" Lees spat. "I know all about ye, John Newton. A lot like me, ye is."

"Once, yes," John said, blushing with shame. "But not anymore. God—"

"God!" Lees sneered. "How convenient. Too scared to die, so ye got religious."

John gazed thoughtfully at Lees. To his great sadness, he *did* see a lot of himself in the man. "Afraid to die and face God in my sin, yes. If that's what you mean."

"So now ye's the great holy man!" Lees scoffed. "Well, we'll see 'bout that."

The *Duke of Argyle* sailed from Africa with 174 slaves. After two days at sea, Ted Burke, sprawled across the deck in his chains, sunburned and mosquito-bitten, called for the captain. " 'Twas a fool thing I done, Sir," he said. "Forgive me, I beg ye." His punishment ended that day.

Lees, however, feverish and rambling, raised his voice and ranted about yet another mutiny plot. It was to take place in the Middle Passage. All officers would die, he said, and Lees would take command of the *Duke of Argyle*.

"Yes," Burke confirmed, "it's all true. That's just how Will has it planned."

The next morning, when a warship sailed into view, Captain

John Newton ordered, "Hail her and offer to make a trade. I want Lees off this ship."

That evening, a line of young slave women, washed and dressed up in clothes from a chest of dresses kept for just such an occasion, cowered together and struggled to keep the half-drunken sailors at bay. But they were helpless against the blatant advances. Men swept up one young girl after another and carried her kicking and screaming to the sleeping quarters below. John turned away and walked alone to the bow. Gazing up at the sparkling stars spread across the velvet expanse of sky, he prayed long into the night, asking God for strength to control what he called his "improper emotion."

Deep in the hold, the tight packed captives listened in anguished silence to the course, drunken laughter overhead, punctuated by screams and cries from their women. It wasn't until the wee hours of the morning that Seamen Burke and Noble, both much the worse for drink, stumbled downstairs, and, fumbling with the chains, locked the women back into their places.

"Whoooeee, that were some party!" Burke exclaimed. Then to the women whose manacles he was securing: "You all get a good sleep."

But Noble interrupted him with a blast of expletives. "*%#! I dropped the keys!" he said. "I ain't muckin' around in this filth!"

"We'll find them tomorrow in the daylight," Burke said. "Come on. I can't stand the stink down here any longer!"

The two stumbled back up the ladder and thumped the hatch door down behind them, plunging the hold into darkness. A sprinkling of sobs. Then, a scratching . . . and a rattle. And then a clink as one man's chains fell to the deck. Another clink, then another and another and another. . . .

"Rebellion!" the cry rang out. John, forcing himself awake,

struggled to sit up. Simon Andrews was pounding on his door. "Captain!" he yelled. "The Africans are out!"

Jumping from his bed, John pulled on his pants and grabbed for the door. "Bolt the hatch! Don't let them up on deck!"

"Too late, Sir! Deck's already swarming with them!"

When John reached the top of the ladder, he was immediately surrounded by a mob of angry black men, their legs still bound in chains. Two lunged at him, brandishing knives and shouting in a language he couldn't understand.

"Simon! The whips!" John cried.

One hundred seventy four desperate captives with nothing to lose against twenty-eight men taken by surprise while sound asleep. A fight for life, it was . . . and for the survival of the ship. A slave leapt onto John's back and grabbed him by the throat. But at that moment a whip cracked through the air, slashing him off. With Jason Cunningham and Simon Andrews in the lead, half a dozen sailors advanced on the captives, lashing whips and forcing the slaves toward the hatch door. But 174 to 28—it was obvious that whips alone couldn't hold them all back. Sure enough, with a sudden roar of rage, the Africans surged forward.

"If they get the whips they'll use them against us!" Dr. Mann warned.

"The guns!" John ordered. "Shoot every slave on this deck! If we have to, we'll kill every woman and child in the hold, too!"

Soon the air was grey with smoke. When it cleared, bodies lay strewn across the deck. And still Africans kept coming. Some, the crewmen shot. Others raised their hands in surrender. Captain John Newton, his face distorted with rage, ordered, "Take them below and lock them up! No food for any of them today or tomorrow. And for the rest of the trip, half rations!"

That was just the beginning. After clamping heavy, excruciating metal collars around the men's necks, the crew locked them in irons. For any suspected of master-minding the rebellion, John ordered thumbscrews, tightened until the Africans screamed for mercy and confessed to anything that would end the torture.

"Savages, that's all they are!" Andrews grumbled with disgust. "Not the least regard for any of us."

"Can't treat them like human beings," Dr. Mann agreed. "First chance they get, they'd slit our throats."

"Hmmmm," John mused. "Some of my own crew, who are supposedly civilized white men, would do the same if they could."

Although no one liked the job, Jason Cunningham gathered a group of reluctant sailors and put them to work sewing the dead into their hammocks in preparation for burial at sea. When he signaled John that the job was done, the captain summoned the crew to the deck. Solemnly he recited the Lord's prayer, and a smattering of men joined in. After calling out the name of each white man who died, John said, "We commit their bodies to the deep, where they will await the day when the sea shall give up the dead in the day of the resurrection." He took off his hat and bowed his head, and the others did the same. Then one by one, Simon Andrews slid the shrouded bodies into the ocean.

Little was said that day. Andrews kept his distance from the captain and spoke only when directly addressed. Late in the afternoon, as he inspected the damage on deck, John walked by. Simon didn't look up. John stopped right in front of him, but still his first mate ignored him. Finally John said, "I would think you'd be overjoyed at the outcome of our adventure, Mr. Andrews. Yet you seem disapproving. Perhaps you would prefer it be us at the bottom of the ocean and the Africans sailing the ship?"

"I would prefer you not make our voyage completely worthless," Andrews said.

"And what do you mean by that?"

Andrews looked his captain in the eye. "We buried three of our men at sea, Sir. The ship is badly damaged. We lost a great deal of valuable cargo. And now, to get even, you are starving the rest."

"You, Mr. Andrews, will never sail with me again!" John snapped.

"You can be sure of that, Sir!"

Actually, John regretted his readiness to provoke an argument, sometimes on the silliest of issues. And once started, his anger would flare out of control. "I must set a stricter guard on my own temper," he wrote in his journal.

Conspiracies against the captain didn't end with Will Lees' departure. Some of the crew still determined to take over the ship and become pirates. They had a plan, too, just waiting the right opportunity. One morning, word was whispered around, "Today is the day!" But before anything could happen, two of the leaders suddenly took ill. When Dr. Mann looked at the first one, he shook his head. "Too late," he said. "This one's already dead." The other men glanced at one another. The plot wasn't mentioned again.

When the *Duke of Argyle* reached Antigua, only sixteen of the original thirty crewmen still lived. Far too many slaves were gone, too. Still, John's share of the profits was 257 pounds, more than three times his wages for his fourteen months as first mate.

In Antigua, John got terrible news—his father was dead. Seems he went for a swim in the icy waters of the Hayes River and drowned. *He did so much for me!* John mourned. *So many chances he gave me.* And, at last, the realization for which he had longed his entire life: *Surely, underneath that harsh exterior, my father truly did love me.* But now . . . oh, so much that could never be said.

"—and I have been doing calculations to determine the most profitable method—" the plantation owner who had given John the message about his father was saying. Suddenly he stopped and gave John a strange look. "Am I boring you?" he asked.

"No, no!" John answered, pulling himself to attention. "Please go on."

"As I was saying, I've been studying the best way to manage slaves. Now, here's the question: is it better business to give them moderate work and sufficient food and clothes so they can live into old age and serve us for many years? Or is it better to rigorously work them to the utmost, with little rest and little food, and wear them out before they become useless and unable to work?"

"What did you find?" John asked.

"Skilled calculations show it's cheaper to work them hard and, when they drop dead, to simply buy new ones to fill their places."

"How long does a slave survive, then?" John asked.

"Three years, four . . ." the plantation owner said. "Longest I ever saw was nine years."

Surprisingly, the man's skilled calculations caused John no pain. Nor did the plight of the slaves who went from his ship onto the auction block in Antigua. Nor even the poor captives who perished in anguish at sea. What did cause him pain was his father's death. And hearing that no letters awaited him from Mary.

"She must be sick . . ." John vexed. "Or . . . maybe she's even dead!"

John worked himself into such a state he could neither eat nor sleep. He feared he had suffered a stroke. Finally it occurred to him to send a boat to St. Kitts Island where the ship was originally scheduled to dock. Sure enough, there was his stack of letters.

John wanted to go home!

# CHAPTER 17

# 1753

*"Though I was very weak, I was sincere in my profession of faith. My imperfection was not my choice, but my greatest trouble. How I pray for God to deliver me!"*

BARELY EIGHT MONTHS AFTER JOHN ARRIVED HOME, JOSEPH MANESTY summoned him to the Liverpool docks to examine his next ship, the *African.* And a fine ship she was, too, beautiful and new.

"As you requested, Sir," Benjamin Boyd, the carpenter, said as he led John to the lower deck to see the "barricado" he had constructed in the slave quarters. The strong wooden wall topped with metal spikes was just the thing to secure captives from the rest of ship. "And that's not all," Benjamin said. "Look here." At intervals, guns pointed inward toward the slave quarters. This time, John was taking no chances.

Being October and the middle of the shipping season, the docks buzzed with activity. Over to one side, a small group of Quakers annoyed people by handing out anti-slavery pamphlets. Every shipping season, a handful of Dissenters came to protest, and every season they were alternately ridiculed and ignored. This time they started to sing:

From north to south the princes meet
To pay their homage at His feet;
While western empires own their Lord,
And savage tribes attend His word.

*Yes!* John thought. *I know those words!* One of Isaac Watts' hymns. John and his mother used to sing it when he was small. Softly, he sang along:

People and realms of every tongue
Dwell on His love with sweetest song. . . .

"Ha! Ha! Getting one of your #%*# mockeries ready, are you?"

Startled, John spun around.

"If it isn't my old mate, John Newton! And a welcome sight you are."

A scruffy sailor . . . vaguely familiar. A rough, loud seaman who had obviously been enjoying his rum even though it was still morning. "Job Lewis?" John guessed. "Is that you?"

"One and the same! You shipping out?"

"I am," John said. "Got my own ship."

"Is that so! Well, Captain, today is your lucky day. I just walked off a worm-eaten tub with the worst #*@! excuse of a captain who ever lived, may his soul rot in hell, so I'm free to give you a hand!"

Job Lewis. The one with the religious heart and the sharp conscious. The good one, with the gentle spirit. What happened to him?

"What's the matter?" Job asked. "You still holding a grudge against me for slicing the ropes on your hammock your last day on the *Harwich?* Come on, you would have done the same to me. In fact, you did much worse to me!"

"You're right," John admitted. "But that was a lifetime ago. And I've changed, too." He then related how God had used the deadly storm to convince him, once and for all, of his utter need of divine grace.

First Job roared with laughter. Then, when he realized John was serious, he broke into the vilest streak of cursing John had heard since the day of the storm. "So maybe I should stand in the rain and pray some magic mumble jumble, and God would make a new ship appear for me," Job mocked. "That how it works?"

*What have I done!* John thought sadly. *He was a good lad before he met me.*

"We sail tomorrow," John told Job. "A captain can't have too many good hands."

Fact was, John already had a full crew. He had no need for another man. But since he had changed Job once by his example, he figured that surely he could do it again. Certainly it was worth the try.

The next morning, Captain John Newton called to the helmsman, "The wind stands fair. We shall not waste it. Set the course—south, south-southwest. We are bound for Africa." But once at sea, John quickly realized how deeply Job had sunk into depravity, rebelliousness, disobedience, and blasphemous profanity.

One of John's greatest joys at sea was enjoying the wonders of God's creation—the endless expanse of sky and ocean, both continually in view. The Quakers' singing at the docks stirred up old memories, and now the songs he learned at the Dissenter church flooded his mind. How he and his mother had enjoyed that new way of worship. At home, they would sing the hymns together, especially those written by Isaac Watts. He was their favorite. As they

came back to him now, those hymns were richer and more meaningful than ever. Alone in the bow of the ship, John softly sang:

> Before the hills in order stood, Or earth received her frame,
> From everlasting Thou art God, To endless years the same.
> A thousand ages in Thy sight, Are like an evening gone;
> Short as the watch that ends the night, Before the rising
> sun. . . .

"A *thousand* ages?" John spun around. It was Job again, smirking . . . mocking. "Sounds like the evening you spent under the cat
getting the skin ripped from your bones! Seems to me I remember the name of God on your lips then, too. Not that you were
singing . . . ."

Job had gotten into the rum barrels, another trick he learned
from John. Only John hadn't done all the drinking himself as Job
did. "Listen, I—"

"Oh, don't tell me," Job interrupted in a loud, boisterous voice.
"You're praying for a big storm to blow up and scare me to God. Or
maybe for a huge whale to jump onboard and swallow me up!"

"No. What I—"

"What you are is a fake, John Newton. Don't forget, I know
you. Maybe you can fool these others, but I *know* you! And before
this voyage is over, I'll see to it that everyone else also knows you
for what you really are."

Thinking back on the old days of debating with reason, John
used every argument he could think of to persuade Job to reconsider his position as a blasphemous infidel. When Job could, he
argued back. When he had no sensible arguments, he simply said
in his ugliest voice, "Congratulate yourself, John. I am what you
made me."

And that's exactly what Job proved himself to be. Not three days out to sea, he whispered around, "Free spirits for everyone tonight!" Taking advantage of John's determination to trust him, Job managed to steal an entire cask of ale. Tom Bennett caught wind of the give-away and alerted John, who confronted Job the next morning.

"A rotten lie!" Job scowled. "If I'd stolen it, I'd have drunk the whole thing myself!"

Since Dobbs and Reese were the ones falling-down drunk, the blame fell on them. And since they couldn't remember the night before, they were in no condition to defend themselves. As the cat lashed their backs, Job stood and watched, grinning wickedly.

"Manning!" Job whispered one day. "You're a smart lad. Want to earn some money?" As Job stood watching, Manning—following his instructions—stole a case of snuff from the officer's supply. Then, also under Job's direction, he sold it to the crew. Manning got a small percent, but most of the money went directly into Job's pocket.

When John confronted Job about constantly inciting the seamen to disobey orders, his old friend simply winked and replied with a jaunty, "Just showing who's in charge!"

For the most part, John remained aloof from the crew. He oversaw the work, but then he spent hours studying Latin and mathematics, and even more time poring over the Scriptures. His personal and active Christian faith made him a most unusual slave ship captain. Besides his own study and prayer time, he read Scripture and the Anglican liturgy to the sailors, and he taught them to pray. Although Job ridiculed John constantly, John determined he would do everything possible to see Job turn his life around.

One Sunday, with the entire crew assembled on deck, John read aloud from the Bible. Few wanted to be there. Bored, they half-listened or dozed as John read from Romans 8: "He spared not his own Son, but delivered him up for us all, how shall he not with him also freely give us all things?"

"He can freely give me something," Job called out. "An extra ration of rum!"

That caught the men's attention. They snickered and chuckled; a few even dared laugh out loud. John looked up and frowned, then deciding it better to ignore the outburst than to call more attention to Job, he continued with the reading. "Who shall lay anything to the charge of God's elect? It is God that justifieth. Who is he that condemneth?"

"I'll tell you who condemneth," Job called. "Every #$*! captain who maketh his men sit in the hot sun and listen to him as he readeth foolishness!"

"Mr. Andrews," John said, struggling to control his rising temper, "please remove Mr. Lewis until he regains control of himself."

"Wait!" Job yelled. "You condemneth me! Who do you think you are, God?"

He was still yelling as Tom, with the help of Benjamin Boyd, managed to force him below and lock him in a storeroom.

Once again, John resumed the reading: "It is Christ that died, yea rather, that is risen again, who is even at the right hand of God. . . ." But it was no use. John had lost control. The men laughed and mocked, calling out coarse comments, until he simply gave up and closed the Bible, then dismissed the men.

John went straight to the storeroom where he found Job stretched out on a cot. "I'll be honest with you," John told him. "When I saw you at the Liverpool dock, my great desire was to redeem myself by redeeming you."

"Save your breath!" Job sneered. "You're nothing but a pitiful hypocrite. Remember, I *know* you!"

"You know what I was . . . a blasphemer. The worst of the worst. But I—"

"You sure as &*#! were, and you taught me well."

As the voyage went on, John had ample opportunity to contemplate Job Lewis' words. An irresponsible drunk who was forever stirring up trouble. Foul-mouthed, blasphemous, rude. . . .

One night, secreted in the ship's forecastle, Job Lewis gleefully passed rum around to a group of grateful sailors bunched around him. "From the captain's own supply," he said. "Not that he would offer it to us."

"That he would not," said Manning. "Capt'n's too righteous for 'is own good."

"What we need on this ship is a reasonable captain," Job said.

"'ear, 'ear!" agreed Manning, raising his cup high. "A reasonable capt'n wot cares about his crew!"

"If we was to kill 'im and take over the ship, no one would blame us," said Reese.

"Blame us?" Dobbs chimed in. "They'd *thank* us."

"You're talking mutiny, you know," said Job.

"Yes! Kill John Newton!" Reese cried in a hoarse whisper. "And Andrews, too. Then you could be our captain, Job. You'd treat us right."

Job leaned back, a satisfied smile spreading across his face. "All we need is someone to do the deed. How about you, Reese?"

"Not me! No, I ain't no killer."

"I'll do it!" Manning suddenly blurted.

Job pulled a knife from the sheath at his belt and handed it to Manning. "If you're going to, now is the time."

Manning grabbed the knife, jumped to his feet, and bounded for the ladder. Suddenly he grabbed his head and crumpled to the deck, moaning. At first, the others stared numbly. But then Reese made his way over to where Manning lay. "He's burning hot!" he called to the others. "Must have the fever."

"Jist like that?" Dobbs asked incredulously.

"Never mind!" Job said. "You going to do the job, or not?" When no one moved, he said, "You going to let the captain keep coddling the Africans until they rise up and slaughter the whole bunch of us? Isn't there even one real man among you?"

Barnes jumped up and grabbed the knife Manning had dropped. But before he could reach the ladder, a wave appeared out of the calm sea, swept over the deck, and washed him away. The others gaped in wide-eyed horror.

" 'Tis a sign, is wot!" gasped Dobbs. "God wants the capt'n left alone!"

With cries of agreement, the men scurried away into the night. Job called out in frustration, "Wait! Dobbs . . . Reese! Anthony! Come back! To #%*#! with you all, you superstitious fools!"

✦

The moment the *African*'s anchor found a hold on the bottom of the bay off the coast of Africa, John ordered his first mate to assemble a crew for the longboat. "Be certain Job Lewis is with me at all times," he instructed Tom. Even this arrangement left John uncomfortable, though. He didn't dare leave Job onboard unsupervised. Yet with his behavior so unpredictable, John would have to constantly be on his guard. Already white men had a most unfavorable reputation on the African Coast—well earned, unfortunately.

"Small pox," the ships' captains whispered among themselves. An infected ship from England brought in an epidemic that all but wiped out the supply of slaves sending the price for a slave soaring to almost 120 bars.

On the very first day, as Job followed John into the slave pens, Job loudly proclaimed, "Look at this worthless, worn-out bunch! Not one worth buying." John warned him to stay quiet and leave the dealing to him, but Job shouted to the African trader, "You're nothing but a cheat, you heathen dog!"

The African trader, his face twisted with disdain, shook his fist and shouted back, "What! Do you take me for a white man?"

"It's true, most of the traders are villains," John told Job that night. "But it's no good telling them so. We still have to work with them, whatever the going price."

The next day, they took the longboat upriver to see a trader John did respect—a rotund half-African, half-Englishman by the name of Harry Tucker. "He's never deceived me," John told Job and Tom. The man's power and influence were legendary. Both Africans and white men feared him. Harry received John and his party royally, laying a lavish meal on a table set with china and silver. Still Job would not stop his foul-mouthed, know-it-all criticism of "cheating traders." Before dinner was even served, John carted him off to the longboat, shackled him, and put him under armed guard. Then John spent the rest of the evening doing his best to mend the damage Job had done.

In things of little importance, John determined early on, he would yield to Job in order to keep the peace. Besides, who was he to condemn? But the time came when he absolutely had to face Job. "I can abide the ridicule and the mockery," he said, "and even your blasphemy. I can make excuses for your disobedience and your treachery. But I cannot bring myself to look at you every day and see what I once was."

"That's the difference between you and me," Job replied. "When you were caught between the devil and the deep blue sea, you ran crying to God. If that happens to me, I'll go down cursing Him—just as you taught me."

That very day a ship approached with its flag flying half-mast. John understood the signal—the captain was dead. The ship—the *Racehorse*—was in bad shape. Still, after some quick inquiries, John made arrangements to buy it as a gift for Job. When John presented it, Job exclaimed, "Ha, Ha! Now I'm a captain! Now I'll do things my way!" Without a word of gratitude, he took charge of the *Racehorse* and set sail.

"We'll take the longboat up and have dinner this evening with Harry Tucker at his home, with his family," John told Tom. "It's quite a way upriver. We may have to spend the night."

"Why would he live so far from the slave hold?" Tom asked.

John laughed. "Harry has seven wives! I'm not sure he knows how many children. Built a whole village on a special island just to house his whole family."

✦

The only place to get decent slaves was at the main Portuguese fortress, Harry told John. So that was where John filled his quota. Armed overseers drove his shackled purchases through the "Door of No Return" to the waiting ship. At John's command, Benjamin Boyd had taken out the shelf he constructed in Liverpool. Now the slaves could be loosely packed, with five feet from floor to ceiling rather than the thirty inches they got with the platform in place. They could actually sit up and stretch and move around.

"That will cut our profit," Tom groused.

"Not necessarily," John replied. "We'll get to the market with healthier slaves. Which means a higher price. Which means more money in all of our pockets."

With the last Africans chained in place and the lower deck secured, the crewmen called sheets and trimmed the sails. But before they weighed anchor, a priest stepped through the doorway. John quickly ordered the plank replaced. "Portuguese fortress," he told Tom. "I forgot about the departing blessing."

The priest boarded the *African* holding his swinging censor high. John removed his hat and bowed his head. A quick snap from Tom Bennett's lash reprimanded the few crewmen who didn't quickly follow suit.

"May God's hand be on this vessel and on all those who sail aboard her," the priest intoned. "May the winds be calm, and may God protect the seamen from attacks by the treacherous heathen on board. In the name of the Father, the Son, and the Holy Ghost, Amen."

Crossing back, the priest returned to the fortress through the door open only to the white man. He took no notice of the misery behind him.

The *African* set sail on a stormy sea. All day and all night, anguished captives cried out in misery and terror as the ship tossed and rolled. Waves slamming against the hull strained the oaken timbers until it sounded as though the ship would surely come apart at the seams. With each wrenching crash, the vessel pitched violently, sending agonizing moans upward from the now-putrid hold. "Lock it down!" Tom Bennett ordered, holding his handkerchief over his nose.

The cries . . . the smells . . . the anguish . . . suddenly John detested slaving.

Still, slaving was his job. His livelihood. But he determined that while the Africans were on his ship, he would set a good example by treating them well.

Just off the Ivory Coast, Tom approached John with his spyglass. "Look starboard, Sir . . . and aft."

John raised the spyglass to his eye and scanned the horizon. Then he stopped and focused the glass, looking hard before slowly lowering it. "The *Racehorse*," he said.

"So it seems."

"Pull in close," John said.

As they approached, he saw that the flag was flying at half-mast.

When John boarded the *Racehorse,* he exclaimed, "It's only been three weeks! What happened?"

The sailors explained that as soon as the *African* was out of sight, Captain Lewis spurned the idea of work. Instead of attending to his duties, he opened kegs of ale and drank . . . and drank. He became violent, terrorizing the crew. And then the fever struck him down. "Full o' anger 'e was," one sailor reported. "Certain 'e was damned forever."

"And a 'orrible death he died, too," said another, "with 'im screaming oaths and claimin' to see the devil comin' to take 'is soul to 'ell."

"We was struck with the 'orror of it all," the first sailor gasped. "But 'e refused to ask fer mercy. No, Sir, 'e would not."

John didn't know what to say. Finally, he simply whispered, "I'm so sorry."

"Maybe you is, but we ain't!" another sailor stated. "An' I ain't scared to say it, neither. I's glad 'e's gone!"

The next day dawned bright and calm. John commanded that the captives be unshackled and brought up on deck. "It's a stinking mess down there," he said. "Dobbs and Manning, gather a crew and clean out the hold."

"Unh, Unh! No!" Manning refused. "I ain't going down there!"

To which John ordered, "The whip, Mr. Bennett."

Before the first mate returned, Manning had a crew assembled and they were on their way down the ladder.

John, who usually managed to stay in excellent health, awoke one morning burning with fever. By evening, he was so bad that both he and the ship's surgeon feared he might not survive to see England again. "Hand me my pen and my journal," he asked. So weak he could barely hold the pen, John scratched out these words: "God—able to save to the uttermost." By the next morning, he was much better, and by week's end, completely well.

On his first slave voyage, the constant cries of the captives so jarred and distressed John he thought the noise would drive him mad. By the second voyage, he considered it but a background nuisance. As he lay in his bunk aboard the *African* listening to the familiar keening wails on his third slave voyage, one haunting cry arose from among the chorus of groans. Almost a dirge, it was. A single voice at first, then one by one, others joined in. As John listened, it wove itself into a tune of heartbreaking beauty. A farewell lament to a land and a life forever lost. For the rest of his life, that melody would echo in his heart. And one day it would help him sing his own story.

Until that moment, it never occurred to John that the cargo packed into the hold of his ship was human beings . . . men and women . . . people with souls.

The crew had grown used to their Sunday ritual of two mandatory services, and to prayer morning and evening. Not pleased, but used to it. Now a new rule: the Africans, too, had required services. Whispering that their captain had surely taken leave of his senses, the sailors watched, bemused, as the hold was emptied and all the slaves herded to the deck in their chains to listen as John read to them from the Bible—in English, which none of the Africans understood

"So God created man in his own image, in the image of God created he him; male and female created he them. And God blessed them, and God said unto them, Be fruitful and multiply, and replentish the earth, and subdue it."

"In the image of God!" Reese spat with disdain. "And the capt'n being so dead set against blasphemy and all! Wot does 'e think that be?"

"Look at 'em," said Dobbs. "Ain't got the first notion wot he's talkin' about!"

"And if they did?" Reese replied. "It's one thing to try to make Christians of us, but they's . . . they's . . . they's heathens!"

Late in the afternoon, with the slaves once again locked securely below decks but before evening prayers, Tom Bennett went to see John in his quarters. "If you'll pardon my saying so, Sir," he began, "I worry that you are too casual with the Africans."

John, looking up from his reading, curtly replied, "You know more about being a captain than I do, Mr. Andrews?"

"No, Sir. But it offends the crew to see them treated more or less as they themselves are treated."

"Oh? And are the crewmen chained together below deck? Have they been taken from their homes and families, and are they headed for the slave markets?"

"No, Sir. But it seems to me that—"

"Mr. Andrews, I would suggest you restrain yourself from imparting your vast wisdom on African cargo until you have experience on a ship of your own. Good day!"

As the *African* sailed the high seas under a blazing sky, Captain

John Newton ordered the hatch to the slave deck opened. "Let some air into the lower deck," he said. "A bit of breeze for them."

Although he worried continually about another insurrection, John insisted that these Africans actually behaved more like children in a family than like slaves in chains and irons. And according to what he read in the Scriptures, he believed God only required him to be a humane trader. Which he was. Not one single slave died on the voyage. No longer did John Newton call them captives, or slaves, or even Africans. He called them men and women. Nevertheless, once he arrived at St. Kitts, he readily sold them to the highest bidder.

It was while John was at St. Kitts that he first met another captain who truly shared his faith: Alexander Clunie, a member of a nonconformist congregation in Stepney and a student of the Bible. Soon the two were inseparable. They met every night, alternately on one ship and then the other, and they talked about the things of God, often until daybreak. Clunie introduced John to the idea of grace. "Undeserved favor of God shown towards man," he explained. And he pointed out the difference between the established church and the Dissenters. "For us, it's vital that one has a personal relationship with Jesus Christ . . . as you yourself have, John." Clunie encouraged John to pray out loud. "See how good it is for you and me to hear each other's prayers?" He also encouraged John to make his profession of faith more public. "Don't be afraid to speak up for God. Your experience can be a great encouragement to others."

At long last John had someone who could answer his questions. He had always lived in great fear of losing his salvation because of the enormity of his sin. "Oh, no," Clunie insisted. "You were saved by grace. You are now, and you forever will be, held safe by an unchangeable Savior." John told Clunie of his frustration that despite his greatest efforts, he could not remain sinless. "You're not preserved by your own power," Clunie said. "You're preserved by the power and promise of God."

John arrived in Liverpool in August, secure in his faith for the first time, and totally amazed by the grace of God.

## CHAPTER 18

# 1754

*"I did not at the time start with horror at my employ-
ment in this vile traffic. Custom, example, and interest
had blinded my eyes. Had I thought of the slave trade
then as I have thought of it since, no considerations
would have induced me to continue in it."*

"Congratulations!" Joseph Manesty called out to John. "Not
one slave lost! I don't believe anyone has ever accomplished such a
feat before."

To his amazement, John found that he was the talk of the town.
He was still receiving congratulations when Manesty announced
another ship was ready and John could start fitting it out as soon
as possible.

So little time at home!

As John and Mary sat together enjoying a cup of tea, John said,
"It's genteel employment, my dearest. The occupation God gave
me." Outside, the trees showed the first glimmer of fall. Sighing,
John added, "Although I must admit, I do feel myself a sort of jail-
er. Sometimes I'm shocked to realize I couldn't do my job without
chains and bolts and shackles. Still, the important thing is—"

Suddenly the cup tumbled from John's knee and clattered to
the floor. Then John fell with a thud.

"John!" Mary screamed. Frantically she tried to revive her unconscious husband, but he was barely breathing. Panic-stricken, she ran out the door screaming, "Help! Help! My husband is dead!"

He wasn't dead, of course, but he was unconscious for almost an hour. And when he finally revived, he suffered for days from dizziness, blurred vision, and severe headaches.

"The hot African climate is to blame," the doctor said after checking John over. Then he said to John, "If you want my advice, never go back. You won't survive another trip. Your slaving days are over."

After the doctor left, Mary came to sit by John. Taking her hand in his, he said, "It's strange. In my prayers, I've been asking the Lord if, in his own time, he might fix me in a more humane calling."

"Well," Mary said, "I guess he answered your prayer."

By the day, John's health improved. He felt bad about leaving Joseph Manesty without a captain, but that post was readily filled, and the *Bee* sailed as scheduled.

Mary, however, was so traumatized by seeing her husband on the floor so near death that she suffered a nervous breakdown. For eleven long months she suffered, and no medicine or treatment seemed to help.

One day a young man banged on John's door. "Mr. Newton!" he called. "Mr. Newton, did you hear the news?" John rushed to open the door. "The *Bee* was overtaken by slaves!" the breathless fellow exclaimed. "Killed the whole crew, they did. Threw them all overboard. The captain who took your place is dead."

That evening, John sat beside Mary's bed, stroking her hand. "The truth is, I found the trade increasingly disagreeable," he told her. "I should have quit long ago. It's wrong, my dearest. It should be unlawful."

Over the winter, John and Mary stayed with friends in London and Chatham. And although he didn't have a job, John was anything but idle. A unique opportunity to nurture his religious life—that was how he saw it. He sought out the Christian friends Captain Clunie referred to him, and before long, he was on intimate terms with Mr. Brewster of Stepney. Like a starving man at a lavish buffet, he couldn't get enough of the great preaching in and around London. Anglicans, Baptists, Independents, Presbyterians, Methodists, Congregationalists, Moravians—he went to hear them all. One Sunday, after hearing Charles Wesley preach, John told Mary, "He has such a loving and earnest spirit." Mr. Johnson, a Baptist minister, so impressed John that he would have joined with the church except that he saw no need to be baptized by immersion.

The eighteenth century was an exciting time to be an evangelical Christian! Early one morning, John took his lantern and followed streams of people to the great Tabernacle to hear George Whitefield, just back from preaching in America. The Tabernacle— really a huge barn—had room for over five thousand people, yet hundreds were turned away. This despite the fact that Whitefield held his services at four o'clock in the morning so working people could attend and still be at their jobs on time. They worshipped with heart and soul, joyfully singing gospel songs and soaking up the sermon until daylight. How different from the staid worship in the formal state church.

"It's like a foretaste of heaven!" John told Mary.

Before long, church leaders heard about John Newton and his extraordinary story, and they invited him to speak. "The Lord looked at me with mercy," he would say, "and he did not strike me to hell as I justly deserved." People who heard his words gasped at the amazing grace God showed to a wretched slave ship captain.

Many of John's friends strongly disapproved of the class of people with whom he mingled at these religious meetings. "Poor and ignorant," they said disdainfully. "The lower social classes." Even Mary's family disapproved. "I didn't think my daughter would ever stoop to mix so freely with washerwomen and chimney sweeps!" Mrs. Catlett huffed.

"But we are all brothers and sisters in the Lord," John pointed out.

"Well, you also have brothers and sisters in the Church of England," Mrs. Catlett said. "Why can't you be content with them?"

Later, in the privacy of their own quarters, Mary gently reminded her husband to be gentle. "There is a *way* of doing things. It isn't necessary to affront or quarrel."

Since John would no longer be going to sea, he needed to find another job. In 1755, Joseph Manesty used his influence to get John a coveted onshore position as a tide surveyor at the Custom House in Liverpool. It was common for ship captains to list only part of their cargo in order to avoid paying the full duty, so it would be John's job to board incoming ships to check for contraband and smuggled goods.

Although John was truly thankful for the appointment, it greatly distressed him to have to leave Mary behind in London. After all the separations they had already endured! But her health was worse than ever, so she insisted he go ahead. She would join him when she could. In August, John found a room to rent in Liverpool, a bustling city of 23,000 people. During his first week on the job, he seized a ship, the goods were condemned, and John got the entire value. Except for being separated from Mary, it was an ideal job. John had his own office, a staff of fifty-five, and four manned rowing boats at his disposal. Plus, he had plenty of leisure time. Perfect for continuing his spiritual pursuits.

When Mr. Whitefield visited Liverpool the next month and preached in St. Thomas' Square, John went to hear him in the morning and was so ecstatic that he invited his landlady to go with him in the evening. The suggestion absolutely horrified the dear lady.

"How can someone who preaches on village greens, in fields and sheds and markets, really be a man of God?" she insisted.

John suggested she come and see for herself . . . which she finally did. She was so moved she bought all of Whitefield's books to read and invited her own friends to come and hear. Then she invited the preacher to her house for dinner.

"You're hurting your reputation by associating with those people," Joseph Manesty warned John. "Genteel society wouldn't think of mingling with them."

Despite the fact that the doctors could do absolutely nothing to help Mary, she began to improve. And on October 18, stronger and healthier than John ever dared hope, she joined him in Liverpool.

One morning, John awoke before dawn and couldn't get back to sleep. Quietly he got up and made his way to the watch-house. He would get some work done early, he decided, then go home, and enjoy a leisurely breakfast with Mary before going back to work. But before breakfast was over, a terrible storm blew in. It wasn't until afternoon that John was finally able to get back to the watch-house.

What a sight greeted him! The roof had been blown off, and the chimney was in shambles. Rushing in to check for damage, John froze. His chair, where he spent most of his time in the office, had been smashed to pieces by the falling chimney.

"In the very place where I thought myself completely safe," John said to Mary that evening. "Surely God favored me with a special grace to deliver me so. I prize that grace more than gold or silver."

CHAPTER 19

# 1757

*"Though I had problems with some tenets of the Church of England, my overwhelming desire was for peace, union, and usefulness."*

"YOU'RE CRAZY, JOHN NEWTON! GIVE UP A WONDERFUL JOB TO GO INTO the ministry? And what are you going to do, serve among *Dissenters?* You have lost your mind!" friend after friend exclaimed.

But John told Mary, "I'm not doing it to please them. I'm doing it to please God."

"Too much emotion in matters of faith," some who watched him whispered. "It can only mean one thing," and here they fairly spat the word: "*Evangelical!*"

"Yes," others agreed. "He claims too much familiarity with God. What does he think—he is already clergy?"

Well, maybe he did involve himself deeply in worship. And, yes, it was true that he prayed from his heart rather than recite official prayers. But John still longed to be ordained in the established Church of England. Problem was, every clergyman he asked to write him a testimonial turned him down. "Methodist!" they whispered behind his back. He applied to the Archbishop of York . . . who sent him to the Bishop of Chester . . . who shook his head, saying John was outside his diocese, so he could do nothing. When John finally did manage to gather the testimonials, he sent them to the Archbishop's chaplain. After a long wait, he received a reply from the Archbishop's secretary stating that canon law ensured an educated clergy, that John didn't have a university education, and that "His Grace was inflexible in supporting the rules and canons of the church."

"It would be wrong to bury my talent in silence just because I have been refused ordination in the established church," John told Mary. "After the great things God has done for me! I'm not the only one feeling this way, either. I know several sensible, godly men in good standing in the established church who grew so tired of being turned down that they struck out on their own as itinerant ministers and—"

"Don't do that!" Mary begged. "Is it up to man or up to God?"

One cool autumn day, John rode to Leeds to hear Reverend Edwards preach. When the service was over and John was ready to leave, Reverend Edwards called, "John Newton! How about you speaking from the pulpit tomorrow?"

"I . . . I don't know—" John hesitated.

"Come, my lad," Edwards urged. "Bring your notes, and you will do just fine."

The more John thought about it, the more he agreed that this might be a good opportunity for him. As for notes, what did he need with them? He knew perfectly well what he wanted to say. He'd rehearsed it a hundred times in his head.

The next evening John stood confidently in the pulpit and started with ease. But before he got far, he stumbled . . . then he lost his train of thought . . . then, hopelessly confused, he had no choice but to give up and sit down. How humiliating!

"Don't worry," his friends consoled when they heard about the debacle. "You can always be an independent pastor."

Mary had another suggestion. "If you want to be ordained in the Church of England, perhaps you should attend some Church of England services."

It made sense. And John did try. But, he finally told Mary, "Nothing in that preaching quickens my faith." Which certainly didn't strengthen his case with the established church. Even so, he was resolute in his desire to be an Anglican minister.

The following April, as the trees were beginning to bud, John visited Yorkshire, where several men urged, "Come, John, share with us." Remembering his humiliation in Leeds, John shook his head. But they urged, "The pulpit is yours. Speak to us."

*Well,* John figured, *if I take my notes with me. . . .*

Standing before the congregation, John buried his face in his notes, and, like a boy just learning to read, he never looked up until his talk was over. Another disaster!

That evening he told Mary, "Unless I can speak warmly from my heart, with God helping me, it will all be in vain."

"Just tell your story," urged John's old mentor Alex Clunie. "A sinner saved by grace. That's your strength."

It was true, John did have a wonderful common touch when he shared himself. Although, not everyone found his story compelling. Tomasin, his stepmother, certainly didn't. "John Newton? A *Christian?* Well, that would be terrible news for the saints!" she mocked. "I know him well, and I'll tell you this: he is making a fool of someone!"

In 1760, at the age of thirty-five, John Newton was invited to pastor an independent church in Warwick. Although he longed to preach for Christ whom he had so dishonored, he said a hesitant no. The Church of England was still his goal.

"Did you hear? The British Royal Navy defeated the French

fleet off the coast of Portugal!" By 1764, victory was all the talk in Liverpool.

"So many have read your letters telling your story of life at sea," Alex Clunie said to John. "I believe that now, in these days of encouragement, is the time to publish them." Within weeks of its August 1764 publication, every copy of *An Authentic Narrative* sold out. People from all over England wrote asking John to help them find God.

"People stare at me after reading these letters," John said. Then he conceded, "and well they might."

One who read the *Narrative* was Lord Dartmouth, a wealthy evangelical Christian—and a powerful man charged with selecting the clergy for the parish church of St. Peter and St. Paul in the town of Olney. He offered the post to John. And at long last John received the message he had long awaited.

"I'm to be in London for my ordination . . . in one hour!" he exclaimed.

John took off running and made it on time to the palace where the exam was to be held . . . only to have the chaplain for the Archbishop of York keep him waiting for two hours . . . only to be told, "No, Sir. We will not consider you."

Not being one to give up, John ran back to the Earl of Dartmouth's home. "Please, sir, I know you are at dinner But I must have a personal note to the Archbishop . . . right now, Sir!" he pleaded. With the note in hand, John ran all the way back again.

Still, it took many more meetings and still more pleadings before he was finally accepted in 1764 at the age of thirty-eight.

When the newly ordained Reverend John Newton preached for the clergymen who signed his testimonials, some were pleased, but most complained with disgust: "Too long!" "Too loud!" "Too extemporaneous!"

"Even so," John told Alex Clunie, "the Lord enabled me to preach his truth before many thousands."

John and Mary packed up their possessions and moved to the small country town of Olney. Nothing special there. Laborers, carpenters, blacksmiths, lace makers, small traders—just ordinary townsfolk, many illiterate.

"A town of factory workers!" Mrs. Catlett sniffed. "Really! I always believed my daughter would live among genteel society. Why, they can't even pay you properly. How are you supposed to live?"

"The Lord will provide," John assured her.

John Newton preached and people came to listen. Many people. All kinds. Not just Anglicans, but Dissenters, too. And the village church grew by the week. When the *Narrative* was first published, John worried that it might make him look vain. But, as he looked out over the crowd who came to see and hear him, he could only shake his head in wonder that a young man who blasphemed God with a filthy mouth, who destroyed the faith of many and barely escaped death so many times, was now a minister in the Church of England.

"It chiefly relates my *misery*," John said. "Had I given details of the *wickedness* of my heart and life, the book would have been too shocking to read."

To John's delight, he found many actively evangelical parishioners in Olney who saw things as Dissenters did, both in relation to scripture and to society. Such things as injustice and inequity. And the abolition of slavery. As for John, his preaching was strongly influenced by George Whitefield and John and Charles Wesley. He may not have felt called to be a Dissenter, but he certainly incorporated his personal convictions into his ministry—an Anglican preacher with strong evangelical leanings.

"You've been to the American colonies," a man called out to John one Sunday morning. "Tell us about the Lord's work there."

"I must admit, I'm not much concerned with the treaties and policies of the kings on earth," John replied. "I long for victories of our King Jesus."

Even so, he never escaped the shadow of the politics of the slave ships. And although he spoke out against ill treatment of slaves, he didn't say a word against slavery itself. It was legal, after all, and an acceptable occupation. Certainly those who benefited from it weren't likely to sit back and listen to him criticize without calling him to accountability for his own misdeeds. Oh, yes, John was the greatest of sinners. He openly admitted it. Still, he cringed at the thought of his horrible past laid out in full detail before those who now looked upon him with love and respect. He was a preacher, after all. Leave the politics to the politicians. If some Evangelicals were influenced by his autobiography to speak out, fine. As for John, he would stick to the grace of God.

Prayer on Tuesdays . . . lectures on Thursdays . . . after-church gatherings on Sundays for prayer and singing (these were so popular John had to issue tickets!). Soon the small church in Olney was crammed with as many as two thousand people each week. They simply couldn't get enough of the ex-sea-captain who preached from his heart, teaching from the Scripture he treasured, and singing the hymns he loved.

"Anyone who walked six miles or more to get to church this morning is invited to dine with my good wife and myself after service!" John announced from the pulpit. "In fact, the invitation is open every Sunday."

A small enough gesture, it seemed. In the first year, however, the congregation outgrew its building, with many of the people coming from afar. John held three services on Sunday—one for children, another for young people and those just beginning in the Christian faith, and a third for more experienced Christians. Still they didn't have enough room.

"I have a gift to you," Lord Dartmouth told John.

And what a gift it was! A mansion the church could use for meetings; "The Great House," was what it came to be known as. Of all the groups that met there, none enjoyed it as much as the children. John loved to sit with the little ones—sometimes as many as two hundred!—and explain the Scriptures in a way they enjoyed and could understand. How he prayed that some of them would grow up to seek the Lord!

Through his friendship with Christian philanthropist John Thornton, Reverend Newton got to know Thornton's sister Hannah Wilberforce. Soon she was coming from London with her young nephew William who lived with her, and the two often stayed at the vicarage with John and Mary.

"Sir," William said one day as he followed along after John. "Were you really a pirate?"

"A pirate?" John laughed. "I was many things, William, but not a pirate. But if you are a very good lad, I'll tell you a pirate tale before you go to bed tonight."

"Yes, Sir!" William said. "And will you make me a paper boat, too? If I am really good and memorize Psalm 23?"

John laughed out loud. What a lad this was! He was constantly on John's heels, asking questions, remembering everything he heard . . . and so quick to learn!

William's mother was not pleased, however. Her sister-in-law's support of the new Methodist movement disturbed her so greatly that she abruptly moved her son back home and cut him off from all of Hannah's friends.

"I do miss the boy," John told Mary. "But even though I don't see him, I will never stop praying for William Wilberforce."

One day a man in John's congregation informed him, "Did you hear about your old friend, Joseph Manesty? His business failed. He's bankrupt."

Bankrupt! That meant John's investments and savings were gone, too. When John told his wife, she only said, "Oh, that dear man! What a terrible time for his family! If only we could do something!"

John knew, though, what had to be in the back of her mind: the growing cost of feeding the ever-increasing crowds around their Sunday dinner table. "The Lord will give us what we need," he gently assured her. "Are his promises not surer than a whole ream of bank-bills? Come, my dearest, let us pray for Joseph."

In Olney, John and Mary met William Cowper, a timid thirty-six-year-old unpublished poet from Cambridge. He had come to know Christ just two years before while a patient in a private mental asylum. At the time, Cowper was unknown, unemployed, and—quite simply—an odd, eccentric fellow. Yet John admired Cowper's humble devotion to God and deep knowledge of the Bible, and he saw him as a blessing to himself and to the entire congregation. William Cowper and Widow Unwin, at whose house he lived, often met with John and Mary at the parsonage to sing hymns around the harpsichord, then to pray together. John and Cowper became such close friends that as long as John pastored in Olney, the two were seldom apart from one another for more than a day.

"The church will no longer hold the crowds that come to hear you," church officials told John. They built on a gallery to seat more people, but soon even that wasn't room enough.

Not that John's growing popularity did anything to still

Tomasin's ridicule of him. But rather than rebuke or ignore her, he simply pointed out, "She has good reason to doubt. She did, after all, know me well." John made it a point to renew contact with his stepmother, and whenever she needed help, he was always there. John's half-brother William was a copy of what John had once been—a debauched, outspoken infidel—and it broke John's heart. Harry, the younger boy, was in Boston with the Royal Navy, and Thomasina, whom John never really knew, was happily married.

In time, Tomasin became a devout Christian. One day she contacted John. Sobbing so hard she could hardly speak, she told him, "Your brother William is dead!" Only thirty years old, an infidel to the end.

On the heels of that sad news, word came that Mary's brother Jack—John's close friend—caught a fever and died within days.

*Life and death,* John mused. *Why William and not me? Why poor Jack? Choices made—free will . . . God's grace—a sovereign God. . . .*

Then, in November 1765, John received a message from George Whitefield in the American colonies. He was opening a university and seminary in Savannah, Georgia. "I would like to offer you the position of president," Whitefield wrote.

Ahhh, such a temptation! A most important position in a most important place. For two days, John closed himself in his study and prayed.

"What did you decide?" Mary asked John when he finally emerged.

"I declined," John told her. "Because of my love of Olney . . . and, my dearest, because of your hatred of the water."

It was a wonderful tribute to John's compelling nature and Mary's warm and accepting home that the vicarage was seldom without guests. Never did they give an indication of the amount of money their hospitality cost them. One day, however, Mr. Thornton took John aside and said, "Keep on being hospitable. And continue to help the poor and needy. I will see that you always have whatever you need." And John Thornton was true to his word.

To the joy of the people and the consternation of the Church of England, John Newton loved including meaningful hymns in his services. Problem was, this being a somewhat newfangled worship idea, he had few from which to choose. So he started writing his own, a new one each Sunday to fit his particular sermon. When his friend William Cowper was well enough, he—being a poet—also wrote hymns.

One bone-chilling day in late December, John worked on a sermon for New Year's Sunday. First Chronicles 17:16–17 was the text he chose: "And David the king came and sat before the Lord, and said, 'Who am I, O Lord God, and what is mine house, that thou hast brought me so far?'" Again and again he read that verse. A new hymn to go with the message . . . a new song to start a new year . . . *Who am I?*

From deep in his memory, a haunting tune stirred . . . a long-ago lament rent from the souls of African captives chained in the hull of his ship. . . .

*What a wretch I was! Oh, but I didn't know! I was so blind . . . It was only God's amazing grace. . . .*

From his own testimony, etched deep on his heart, the words tumbled out:

> Amazing grace! (how sweet the sound)
>> That sav'd a wretch like me!
> I once was lost, but now am found,
>> Was blind, but now I see.

'Twas grace that taught my heart to fear,
 And grace my fears reliev'd;
How precious did that grace appear,
 The hour I first believ'd!

Thro' many dangers, toils and snares,
 I have already come;
'Tis grace has brought me safe thus far,
 And grace will lead me home.

The Lord has promis'd good to me,
 His word my hope secures;
He will my shield and portion be,
 As long as life endures.

Yes, when this flesh and heart shall fail,
 And mortal life shall cease;
I shall possess, within the vail,
 A life of joy and peace.

The earth shall soon dissolve like snow,
 The sun forbear to shine;
But God, who call'd me here below,
 Will be for ever mine.

On New Year's Day 1769, John Newton stood in the pulpit of the church of St. Peter and St. Paul in the small town of Olney, England, and said to an overflow crowd, "Our new hymn for to-day is called *Amazing Grace*." Then, line by line, verse by verse, he taught it to his congregation. Though the words brought tears to his eyes, it was just another hymn. The next week, it would be yet another. *Amazing Grace* didn't even appear in print, except for the *Olney Hymnal*, published eleven years later. It was one of the 280 hymns written by John Newton and 68 by William Cowper. Who could have guessed that centuries later—all around the world and in countless languages—people would still be singing of God's amazing grace to the haunting strains once echoed from the depths of a slave ship?

More and more invitations poured in asking John Newton to come and speak from Oxford, York, even Scotland. And everywhere he went, crowds followed. But if he ever dared show any sign of pride, Mary would lead him to his study and point to the verse painted above the fireplace: "But thou shalt remember that thou wast a bond-man in the land of Egypt, and the Lord thy God redeemed thee." (Deuteronomy 15:15)

In January of 1771, a messenger stomped the snow from his boots and rapped briskly on the vicarage door. John read the note, then said sadly, "It's Joseph Manesty. He died last week."

His dear friend and benefactor. Another important piece of his past, gone.

On March 21, John retired to his room where he spent the entire day meditating and praying, just as he did every year on the anniversary of the ship wreck that changed his life. "That awful, merciful, never-forgotten day, when a storm revealed God's grace to me." He kept the practice for the rest of his life. "For on that day, the Lord sent a storm from on high and delivered me out of the deep waters."

John filled his days with preaching . . . and throngs of people . . . with friends and family . . . and Bible study and prayer. "You might find richer people than these," he insisted happily, "but none who would love you better." But at night, shrouded in shadows and quiet, the anguish of African captives rose up to haunt his dreams. Despairing young men in chains, passed once again through the Door of No Return. Babies, worthless to the traders, dashed to death all over again for the crime of helplessness. Human beings, created in God's image, thrown overboard—night after night. The past weighed hard on him, yet John still didn't openly preach against the trade as some Dissenters did. In crying for England's repentance, John Wesley insisted the slave trade was the country's worst crime of all.

"My sins are too heavy, far too numerous to count. I couldn't be saved except by grace—amazing grace—grace greater than all my sins!"

Sins of the past, freedom through grace. Hard, but wonderful beyond words. To John Thornton, Reverend Newton wrote, "All I asked for was a little dissenting congregation in some obscure corner. And look what the Lord gave me! I am so unlike that poor slave of slaves who wandered almost naked, and like a hungry dog was glad to receive a morsel of food from any hand that offered it!"

In the privacy of his own home, John confided to William Cowper many stories of the old slaving days. "The trade is evil," he would say passionately. "The things being done . . . sinful. Just sinful!" John had no idea how deeply all this affected his friend until Cowper began penning poetry critical of the trade. With great talent and stirring passion, Cowper wrote that every person on earth is a sinner before God. Both black and white. And yet everyone is capable of receiving his redemption through grace. Both black and white.

One cold April morning in 1773, John and Mary were awakened long before dawn by persistent pounding at their door. "It's four o'clock!" John said as he stumbled to answer it.

One of Widow Unwin's serving girls stood shivering outside. "'urry, Sir!" she cried. "It's Mr. Cowper. 'E's out of 'is mind, 'e is!"

Cowper's returning madness both alarmed and grieved John. After years of calm, the illness attacked with a vengeance, leaving the poor man depressed and shaking with terror, overtaken with horrifying hallucinations and determined to kill himself. Medicines only made him worse. "My soul is among lions," he told John. "I have temptations that spread gloom over everything. Sin is my burden."

"I think he must move in with us until he's out of danger," John told Mary. Both she and Widow Unwin agreed. What none of them could know was that Cowper wouldn't be well enough to leave for fourteen months.

Shortly after Cowper went back home, Mary's brother George, a widower, died suddenly leaving his sweet five-year-old daughter, Betsy, alone. "Let's adopt her," Mary said to John. "Finally we can have a child of our own!" John enthusiastically agreed.

In a time of bitter religious divisions—established Church of England versus Independent, Calvinist versus Arminian, Catholic versus Protestant—John Newton earned a reputation as the Great Uniter. "I am an avowed Calvinist, by Scripture, reason, and experience," he once said. "Yet I feel much more union of spirit with some Arminians than with some Calvinists. And if I thought a person feared sin, loved the word of God, and was seeking after Jesus, I wouldn't walk the length of my study to try to convince him of Calvinist doctrines." John didn't preach divisions, and he didn't preach politics.

✦

"Did you hear about Reverend Ryland?" In church circles, everyone seemed to be whispering the latest gossip: the king's messenger reprimanded a clergyman from Northampton for speaking too freely from his pulpit about the American disputes. "He was thrown into Newgate prison!"

Well, John knew one thing to be true: his friend Ryland *was* violently opposed to the American war. Why, Ryland had said openly, "If I were General Washington, I would call my officers together and make them draw blood from their arms, dip their swords into it and swear they would not sheath them again till America had gained her independence." Fine words to share with a friend, but dangerous ideas to proclaim from the pulpit. No, John would keep his political concerns separate from his preaching.

Like it or not, war did come. And beyond all belief, victory for the American colonies. "Our disunion from America is an event of such great importance, so suddenly and irretrievably brought about, that it seems to me like a dream. I can hardly persuade myself it is true. But we must abide by the consequences," John told his congregation. Then he added, "Well, when we get to heaven, all will be well."

In October of the following year, while John Newton was away in London, a terrible fire roared through Olney causing devastating damage. So moved were the hearts of John's friends in London that they quickly collected money for those who had lost everything and sent it back to Olney with John—more than two hundred pounds. Houses could be rebuilt, but for John, the hearts of Olney had changed. Never again was it the same.

Change, everywhere. After the American colonies gained their independence, British civil war went international. For the first time in more than a century, the British found themselves diplomatically isolated, and their outlook gloomy. "Our great fleet returned, having done but little," John lamented. "A war with France and Spain at the door. America gone. Surely the Lord has controversy with this sinful land."

After fifteen years at Olney, church attendance began to decline. "John Newton is too friendly with the poor!" Some raised this old complaint again—more loudly, now that they thought others might be listening. Others insisted, "Love and grace are all well and good when kept in their place, but John Newton is just too lenient toward sinners." The church decided it was time for a change in Olney, too.

"I love this people, and have often wished and prayed to live and die here," John said sadly. But that was not to be. He preached his last sermon there on January 11, 1780. His text was Jeremiah 17:8, "If we have had trials, comforts have more abounded."

Although some felt the church was ready for a change, many people mourned John's leaving. William Cowper lamented, "I walked in the garden this evening and I saw the smoke coming from the study chimney. That used to be a sign that Mr. Newton was there. But it is so no more."

Reverend Bull—like just about everyone else, a friend of John Newton's—preached at Olney after John had left and was amazed at how many crowded in to hear him and stayed to ask about Reverend Newton. To John he said, "They loved you in me."

# CHAPTER 20

# 1779

*"I am not a person of such mighty consequence as you may suppose. Think of the poor wretch who wandered the plantations without shoe, shirt, or friends. I am the same person still."*

JOHN NEWTON GASPED WITH AMAZEMENT AT THE SIGHT OF ST. Mary Woolnoth Church. It was in the very heart of London, just a few yards from the Bank of England and the Royal Exchange, on Lombard Street, no less—the opulent address of financiers and bankers. Imagine the type of people who must attend such a church!

"Oh, I'm not qualified to minister here," he insisted.

"You most certainly are!" replied John Thornton, who led the committee charged with showing him around. "You're famous now, so you will attract many to the services. Oh, one more thing—this is one of the few large established churches dominated by Evangelicals."

Now fifty-four, John Newton was showing his age. Even without his wig, his formerly raven hair was white, and his creaking joints caused him so much pain he had trouble walking. Sometimes he could hardly rise from a chair without help. John looked around at the hurry and smoke and grit of the busy city. No peaceful woods here. None of the green fields and gurgling streams he so loved. Mary preferred the quiet of Olney. Betsy, too. They would miss the singing of the birds and bleating of the lambs as much as he would.

John located a comfortable home for his family in Charles Square, and before he sent for Mary and Betsy, he walked all around it, trying to picture their new life in the heart of London. Suddenly he stopped and stared. Behind the house, out beyond the backyard, was a small field, complete with trees and cows grazing. "Cows, fields, and birds!" John exclaimed. "It's a sign to me! We shall be at home here. And very happy."

In the bustling financial center of London, Reverend John Newton was the same humble, devout, and useful man he had been in Olney, completely unspoiled by attention from the great and wealthy. In truth, some parishioners of St. Mary's were pleased with what he had to say, and others were not, for it was a congregation made up of various groups which—truth be told—did not get along well. As it turned out, a non-political man in the pulpit was most acceptable. Soon so many strangers flocked to hear John preach that the parishioners either complained that their seats were taken or that they couldn't get to them because the aisles were clogged with people.

"Why don't you take more time off, Reverend Newton?" some suggested. "Maybe then fewer people will come to church."

✦

On the evening of June 5, 1780, with smoke seeping in around the window jams, John threw his back door open and gazed with alarm at the mob on the street. They had been gathering for several days, but tonight people were restless and agitated. He watched in horror as a bonfire suddenly flared up and roared out of control. Then another blazed up, then another and another, showering the entire area with burning embers. ". . . four . . . five . . . six . . . seven fires!" he counted. Already, some licked at the edges of neighboring houses.

"It's Lord Gordon!" John growled. By passing the Roman Catholic Relief Act, Parliament had officially repealed much of Great Britain's legal discrimination against Catholics. Sure, the act was more a matter of expediency than benevolence—the government needed Catholics in the military to help in the ongoing battles with France, Spain, and America—but Lord Gordon was passionate in his insistence that the act be repealed. An articulate—albeit eccentric—propagandist, he inflamed the mob by terrifying them with stories of Catholics in the military joining forces with their Catholic counterparts in France and Spain, then together attacking England.

"If the military hadn't arrived on the third night, I think London would have been in ashes," John later told Mary, who fortunately was in the country with Betsy during the riot. Yet he didn't blame the people. "I believe multitudes followed innocently, unaware of the consequences," he insisted. The evening after the riots he preached to his terrified congregation from Lamentations 3:2, "It is of the Lord's mercy we are not consumed."

John deplored the state of the times. "The cloud grows darker, the flames of war spread wider, and difficulties seem to be increasing against us on every side. The Lord's hand is lifted up, and men will not see," he said. "What a mercy to know who is at the helm."

It was just what people needed to hear in that time of strife. Educated, intelligent Christians crowded together—Anglicans next to Dissenters, Calvinists and Arminians together, Methodists and Moravians, even Catholics and Quakers—all listening to John Newton preach the truth of hope in Christ. And they all returned to their homes with a new understanding of God's truths.

John Wesley, who didn't always agree with Newton theologically, once wrote him a letter stating, "You appear to be designed by divine providence for a healer of breaches, a reconciler of honest but prejudiced men, and a uniter (happy work!) of the children of God."

John Newton understood people. Even more, he had an unusually clear grasp of God's grace and mercy. Neither of these came through scholarly training but through personal experience.

Sermons alone were not enough. John was known for the multitude of letters he wrote to both dear friends and casual acquaintances, offering comfort, joy, instruction, and even correction. After many requests, he published several volumes of his letters: *Omnicron,* then *Cardiphonia* (Greek for utterances of the heart), and later *Apologia.* Widely circulated, they made him known and appreciated throughout the religious world.

John also held monthly services at homes in London. Hannah Wilberforce was one who attended regularly. In fact, John presented a series of lectures on *Pilgrim's Progress* at her house, which is how he kept up with the progress of her nephew, William. John continued to pray for the boy, especially during his years at Cambridge. (Everyone seemed to know about young Wilberforce's student years of parties, gambling, and drinking, though, as his aunt stressed, "He isn't nearly as bad as many of the other students!") John was still praying for William when, at the age of twenty-one, the young man ran for election to parliament in 1780. Four years later, when Hannah shared that he had converted to evangelical Christianity, no one rejoiced more than John Newton.

"Social reform," Hannah said. "That's what interests my nephew. Especially abolishing the slave trade."

Actually, more and more people were in favor of doing away with slavery. Still, for every one in favor of it, hundreds more wanted the trade left alone. And why not? It was good business. A full fifty slaving ships operated from the Liverpool port. Without the slightest blush, people boasted that every stone and brick of its buildings were cemented with the blood of slaves. Everything that made Liverpool great and grand was due to the slave trade. And not only Liverpool, either. It was the same all over England. Hundreds of members of Parliament, tucked securely into the pockets of slavers. Anyway, the vast majority of slaves were far away in the Caribbean, or Brazil, or America. Well away from the eyes and sensibilities of the genteel British public.

Until the incident with the *Zong*, that is. The British captured the Dutch slave ship in 1781. Hungry for profits, far more slaves had been packed aboard than the ship could possibly handle. With seven crew members and sixty Africans already dead, and the other slaves sick and hungry, Captain Collingwood decided to throw the whole lot over and be rid of them. Simply lost cargo. If they went over alive, the Liverpool ship owners could file an insurance claim, but not if they died on board. So Collingwood gave the order. That day 133 slaves drowned.

When word reached England, it spread fast.

"Could it be true?" horrified women gasped to one another over stacks of apples and cabbages in the marketplace.

"A *British* ship? Is it possible?" men asked over their tankards of ale.

"But we are a civilized society," men argued in their parlors and gentlemen's clubs and places of business. "If it could happen on a British ship . . . well. . . ."

In John Newton's mind, no questions prowled. Only memories. Fellow human beings, they were. God's own children! How it disgusted him that he was ever a part of that abhorrent business.

"Oh, Lord God," John prayed, "forgive me! But don't ever let me forget."

As always, John proclaimed God's amazing grace from the pulpit. And as he so often did, he used himself as a prime example: "I can see no reason why the Lord God singled me out for mercy unless it was to show, by one astonishing instance, that with him nothing is impossible!" But now, for the first time, he began to add another element to his preaching: "All people, black and white, are created in the image of God."

"You're the poet, my friend," John said to William Cowper, who had recently moved to a mansion outside London to be near John and Mary. "You can inspire people who will never listen to a preacher." Following John's suggestion, Cowper wrote the poem *Charity*, in which he denounced the slave merchant who "grows rich on cargoes of despair." In it he stated:

> A Briton knows, or if he knows it not,
> The Scripture placed within his reach, he ought,
> That souls have no discriminating hue,
> Alike important in their Maker's view . . .

The poem quickly grabbed the nation's attention and became extremely popular.

✦

Throughout the Newtons' life together, Mary's health was always precarious. Since the day John dropped to the floor unconscious, his tea cup lying in pieces beside him, Mary had never been quite the same. The shock was too great. For ten of their forty years together, she was unwell. Often she found it necessary to take Betsy and go stay with friends or relatives in the country, where the pace was slower and the air fresh. Those times were lonely for John. He missed his family.

One May morning when Mary and Betsy were away, John, feeling very much alone, headed for the church. Trees just beginning to burst into bloom in Charles Square reminded him of the country scenes he had so loved in Olney. "So often surrounded by noise, smoke, and dust," he sighed. "Oh, how I long to spend a day or two among woods and lawns and brooks and hedgerows, to hear the birds sing in the bushes, and to wander among the sheep and lambs. To stand under the shadow of an old oak upon a hilltop! But no! Olney was the place once. London is the place now."

In 1783, when Betsy was fourteen, Mary's widowed sister fell terribly ill. She wrote Mary and John, asking if her twelve-year-old daughter Eliza Cunningham could come and live with them.

"A sister!" Betsy exclaimed. "We will have so much fun together!"

Eliza was such a sweet girl that everyone loved her immediately. "She has made herself ours and taken possession of a large room in each of our hearts," John wrote to the girl's mother. "Her affectionate, obliging, gentle behavior has endeared her very much to us. As to her health, she has too much of a fever, though I think she is better since she came."

Two months later, when Mrs. Cunningham died, John and Mary adopted Eliza. Both loved her dearly. But Eliza was always sickly, which meant Mary and the girls were away from the city more than ever.

✦

One Sunday evening, while John was alone in the vestry, a young man came to the door and handed him a letter. "Sir, this is of great importance," he said. Then he was gone. The message was from William Wilberforce, who had been elected a member of parliament for Yorkshire. He was requesting an appointment with John. On the following Wednesday, under cover of darkness, Wilberforce knocked at John's door in Charles Square. "I heard you preach," Wilberforce said when John answered. "I need to talk to you . . . in secret."

Of course in secret. Someone of his stature wouldn't want to be seen seeking advice from an *Evangelical!* Sixty-year-old John grabbed the hand of the former little lad he hadn't seen for so many years, marveling to see him now as a twenty-six-year-old man. "I've never stopped praying for you, William," John said. "Please, do come in."

Sunk deep in spiritual crisis, Wilberforce poured out his desperate longing to return to the faith he once knew. "I have already written to my friend, Prime Minister William Pitt, and explained that if I'm going to live for God I must leave politics," he said. "But I have a thousand doubts. Are wealth and power truly ungodly? Will God only be pleased if I turn away from the world and join a monastery? Or the clergy, perhaps? Or become a missionary?"

John considered the young man before him—talented, wealthy, powerful. The topic of conversation at every society gathering. A friend of royalty. "My dear lad," John said, "God has indeed given you a rare gift. He brought you to a position of national influence so that you can do good. Many men can preach, William, but few can affect the heart of a nation. God can use you in politics. And we need you there, serving your nation while you serve your God."

When William Wilberforce returned home, it was with a whole new sense of purpose. He wrote in his diary, "God Almighty has set before me two great objects: the suppression of the slave trade and the reformation of morality."

When God calls a person to do his purpose, he seldom calls that one person alone. For the next twenty years, John Newton tirelessly mentored the committed young MP. Wilberforce also worked closely with the Clapham Group, people committed to Christ and to the abolition of slavery—Thomas Clarkson, Granville Sharp, Hannah Moore. Some of them had long been in the fight against the slave trade.

John Newton, though, had something the others didn't have—first-hand experience. "I hope it will always be a subject of humiliating reflection to me that I was once an active instrument in a business at which my heart now shudders," he confessed.

John could speak directly on the atrocities of the slave trade, and with authority on its total unacceptability by Christian standards, precisely because he had personally been a part of it. And at St. Mary's, he had the ear of some of Britain's most influential citizens.

"Mr. Wilberforce," John stated from the pulpit on Sunday, "because of your redemption, you have provided our nation with an opportunity for redemption."

✦

Yet it was in John's "dearest" and his two adopted daughters that he found great joy and solace. But Eliza's health was a constant concern. In 1785, Mary suggested, "Perhaps if I took her to Southampton for the summer, the fresh air and the seashore might help her."

Certainly it was worth a try. So although it meant another long absence from Mary and the girls, John agreed.

"I long to hear that Eliza has been in the water and it agrees with her," John wrote to his family. And to Mary alone, "You are dearer to me than all earthly things." He was overjoyed to welcome them back home in September. But already Eliza was sick again.

"Do not weep for me, dear Aunt," Eliza said to Mary who never left the girl's bed. "Rejoice. For I am truly happy." Eliza died the next day. She was just fourteen years old.

"The Lord sent that beautiful child to us to be brought up for him," John said through his tears. "When her education was completed, he took her to heaven. He has paid us richly for our efforts. Blessed be the Lord."

✦

It was the following year that John suggested William Cowper write a song for the Society for the Abolition of the Slave Trade. "That would be just the thing to promote its cause," he said. He was right. Cowper's moving ballad, "The Negro's Complaint"—printed in newspapers across Britain—soon became the rallying cry of the antislavery movement:

> Forc'd from home and all its pleasures,
> Af'ric's coast I left forlorn;
> To increase a stranger's treasures,
> O'er the raging billows borne;
> Men from England bought and sold me,
> Paid my price in paltry gold;
> But, though theirs they have enroll'd me,
> Minds are never to be sold.

More songs followed, and poems, too. Cowper's blistering satire condemned the slave trade and warned of God's judgment. But it would take much more than songs and poems to change something in which so many powerful people had such a vested interest.

One chilly October night in 1787, John sat by the roaring fire in the Wilberforce sitting room, deep in discussion with William. "But how can I gain the support I so desperately need from the wide range of people with whom I must work without compromising my Christian faith?" Wilberforce asked his mentor.

The two talked long into the night. So moved was John by their conversation that when he got home he wrote to the young MP, listing some guiding principles. He summed it up with this: "If you meet with unkind reflections and misrepresentations from men of unfeeling and mercenary spirits, you will bear it patiently when you think of Him who endured the contradiction of sinners against Himself."

The eager group of reformers and Christians who had been carrying on the abolition campaign had not gotten far precisely because they had no access to the men in power. "You are the answer," John told Wilberforce. A young dynamic Christian. A passionate speaker with the ear of Prime Minister Pitt. Yes, William Wilberforce *was* the answer. "The Lord has raised you up for the good of His church and for the good of the nation," John said.

And while John Newton was influencing William Wilberforce, William Wilberforce was influencing John Newton. "My heart is with you in this fight, but I'm too old to actively campaign," John insisted.

"Your writing," Wilberforce pointed out. "It greatly influences public opinion." So, inspired by the young man he was mentoring, in 1788 John Newton published a ten thousand-word essay entitled

*Thoughts Upon the African Slave Trade* that began with Matthew 7:12, "All things whatsoever ye would that men should do to you, do ye even so to them: for this is the law and the prophets."

Cruel, he called the trade. Oppressive, destructive, disgraceful, unlawful, and just plain wrong. John argued that those so brutal to others were in turn themselves brutalized by the experience, and that everyone involved in the trade—from agents to slave ship captains, from slaves to merchants—was debased. And he didn't just say it; he gave specific evidence, writing; "Experience and observation of nine years would qualify me for being a competent witness upon this subject." He told of ordinary Englishmen changed into callous barbarians—raping young girls, torturing slaves, and a sailor who threw a baby overboard because he was upset by its crying. He wrote, "I know of no method of getting money, not even that of highway robbery, which has a more direct tendency to efface the moral sense, to rob the heart of every gentle and human disposition, and to harden it like steel." And he insisted, "for the suppression of a traffic, which contradicts the feelings of humanity, that it is hoped, this stain of our National character will soon be wiped out. . . . God forbid that any supposed profit or advantage which we can derive from the groans and agonies and blood of the poor Africans should draw down his heavy curse on us."

Distributed by the Anti-Slavery Society, every member of parliament received a copy of John Newton's booklet. Even more, his writings on abolition, through newspaper publication, reached people across the country and helped to change the nation's sensibilities.

For years, the civilized, God-fearing British had convinced themselves that black Africans were happier as slaves of enlightened Englishmen than as free heathens, and that the British were doing their slaves a favor by giving them a chance to convert to Christianity and gain heaven. But John Newton held up the truth—the pitiful image of anguished slaves moaning in chains . . . dying horribly . . . dumped callously into the ocean. With this booklet, John gave the abolitionist cause its mightiest weapon. Wilberforce himself distributed thousands of copies to a shocked and horrified nation.

"It's not that we don't have a responsibility to introduce those in far away lands to the gospel," Wilberforce said to John. "Not just Africans, either. But in India. And those in Australia who served their prison sentences in New South Wales."

"And lived to tell about it," John replied.

Still, it was John Newton's words about the African slave trade that tore people's hearts away from the arguments of the politicians and businessmen. "It is righteousness that exalts a nation, and wickedness is the present reproach, and will, sooner or later, unless repentance intervene, prove the ruin of any people," John proclaimed. "The slave trade was always unjustifiable, but inattention and interest prevented for a time the evil from being perceived. . . . Not now. The evils connected with it have of late been represented with such undeniable evidence that I suppose there is hardly an objection that can be made to the wish of thousands, perhaps of millions, for the suppression of this trade except on the ground of political expediency."

But then political expediency was the backbone of power. That, and money: "Even if I were convinced that a major amount of the public treasury depends on the African trade—which I am convinced is far from the case—and if I had access and influence, I should be bound to say to the government, to Parliament, and to the nation, 'It is not lawful to put the money into the treasury because it is the price of blood.'"

Two-thirds of Manchester's male population signed a petition demanding an end to the slave trade. From all over Britain, letters poured in about John's story—not only from England, but from Scotland and America, and even as far away as India.

$$\maltese$$

In 1788, on a bitterly cold April day, John was called upon to serve as pall bearer at the funeral of his long-time friend, Charles Wesley. Throughout the burial at Marylebone Church, John stood in the falling snow, and he came home sick and miserable. It was just at this time that Mary discovered a lump in her left breast.

"I don't want to tell John," she insisted to the doctor. "He has more important things on his mind. I'll just have the surgery and he'll never need to know."

But the doctor shook his head. The cancer was far too advanced for surgery, he insisted. "Just stay as quiet and peaceful as possible. When the pain becomes too great, I will give you laudanum."

That night, with John bundled in blankets and settled before the roaring fire, Mary calmly told him what the doctor said.

Before they had time to mourn, Betsy came down with a fever so terrible that several times they were certain she was gone. Mary was beside herself, far more distressed than she was by her own condition. Next to each other, Betsy held the dearest place in both their hearts. The girl survived, but Mary grew worse. In time, her pain, often intense, never stopped. Over the summer she improved enough to attend church a couple of times, but most of her days were spent in bed reading the Bible. Despite her pain, her spirits were good, and her sense of humor kept John and Betsy laughing.

As John sat with his dying wife, those eager to see the slavery abolition movement fade away took the opportunity to bolster their side of the debate: slavery had always been around, they reiterated; it was as old as the Bible itself. True, the slave trade could be more humane, but that was no reason to condemn the entire process. It did, after all, serve a useful purpose, they reasoned. The entire civilized world benefited from slavery. Consider the price of sugar, cotton, and all the other products kept at a reasonable cost because of slave production. Anyway, they insisted, slaves weren't all that bad off. They had food and clothes, didn't they? And places to live that were far better than the miserable huts of Africa?

"Christian morals, you say?" others mocked. "We've saved those heathens, whether they have souls or not! And as for the good Christian John Newton, why not ask him about his black mistresses? Why not ask how many slaves have Newton blood?"

# CHAPTER 21

# 1790

*"The slave trade was always unjustifiable, but inattention and interest prevented for a time the evil from being recognized. It is not so now. The mischiefs and evils connected with it have been of late years represented with such undeniable evidence, and are now so generally known, that hardly an objection can be made to the almost universal wish for suppression of the trade, save on the ground of political expedience."*

"SO NOW YOU KNOW," SAID REVEREND JOHN NEWTON FROM HIS PLACE in the pulpit of St. Mary Woolnoth Church. "You heard it from my own lips." Sighing, the old man paused to blot a handkerchief across his flushed face. He looked weary. Weary, yet strangely invigorated. And possessed of a renewed resolve.

"I pray to God that I will have the pleasure of standing here before you many more times," he said. "But if I do not—" Here he was interrupted by gasps and whispers, even a few cries of protest. "—If I do not, you will know my loving prayers are with you all."

Already a group of ministers had made the first move toward having him defrocked. An attempt at excommunication would likely follow.

John Newton arrived early at St. James Palace, fully prepared to give his first-hand testimony and answer any questions put to him. The slightly bowed clergyman, pudgy from the fresh-baked hospitality of far too many parishioners, bore no resemblance to the swaggering young foul-mouthed know-it-all slaver of decades past. Years on stinking ships, his own captivity, all the misdeeds and the horror he had regretted for so many years . . . well, had it never happened, he wouldn't be in the unique position to help bring down the terrible trade. *Bringing good out of evil,* John mused. *Isn't that always God's way?*

While John waited to be called, he listened to the testimony of other witnesses speaking in favor of the slave trade. Several talked at length about the many benefits the trade offered the Africans. One went so far as to describe the holds of slave ships as "redolent with frankincense." (Remembering the revolting stink, John had to force himself not to gag.) Another described great fun and laughter among the Africans as they partied on deck, then stated that the passage was "one of the happiest periods of a Negro's life." (*Only compared to the greater horrors to come once they reached the auction block,* John thought grimly.) Samuel Taylor, one of Manchester's largest cotton manufacturers, insisted that the British economy required slave labor; it accounted for 180,000 pounds, he stated, and employed about 18,000 of His Majesty's subjects. ("Blood money!" John hissed under his breath.)

The first person scheduled to speak on behalf of abolition was Robert Norris, captain and merchant. Since he had already been interviewed extensively by the committee, they felt confident he would bolster their case. But once before Parliament, he testified in *favor* of the trade, arguing that it saved Africans from a far worse life in their own country. Evidently, Mr. Norris had been successfully bribed . . . or perhaps threatened.

Furious, William Wilberforce entered the written testimony of a British captain who stated he had thrown 132 living slaves overboard during a storm in order to lighten the ship. When the ship made it back to England, he simply filed an insurance claim for the lost cargo. "The cargo *he* had tossed over board!" Wilberforce bellowed.

And then Prime Minister William Pitt introduced to the assembly the witness both sides had been awaiting—the man who knew the truth of the slave trade from intimate first-hand experience: "The Reverend John Newton." John was escorted into the chamber where King George III sat in his royal box waiting to hear the testimony. First the prime minister, then William Wilberforce, then one peer after the other, rose to his feet in respect.

In a voice strong and deliberate, John told of the marauding raids that provided terrified African captives, of the torture they inevitably suffered as they were forced to walk many miles chained together, of the abuse in the traders' holding stations as the unfortunate Africans waited to be purchased. He described how, once purchased, the Africans were packed in rows on plank benches in the slave ships, "like books on a shelf," shackled hand and foot, unable to turn over or sit up.

"Slave rooms *redolent with frankincense?!*" John exclaimed, his face flushing crimson. "Had my good Sir ever actually been in a slave room, he would know that the smothering heat and noxious, corrupted smell are next to unbearable. Only those fully accustomed to it are able to go down at all."

Calming himself, John continued, "If the slaves and their rooms are constantly aired, and they are not kept on board too long, perhaps not too many die. Unfortunately, the opposite is often their lot. Every morning sailors go below to unshackle the dead from the living, and they toss the bodies of those who didn't make it through the night over the side of the ship. Sometimes nearly one half the slaves on board die before they reach their destination. On the average, one quarter perish."

Then John told of the trader on St. Kitts who had given him the callous calculation: it was more cost efficient to work the slaves to death than to treat them decently and get less production for their money. Endless brutalities . . . whippings . . . tortures . . . all done in the most appalling manner.

"The supposed necessity of treating the Africans in such a way gradually brings a numbness upon the heart and renders those who are engaged in it indifferent to the sufferings of their fellow creatures," John stated. "In treating them as less than human, we become less than human ourselves. How else could we act in so uncivilized, so unchristian, a way?" And then, pointing directly at the esteemed members of Parliament, John Newton dared to state, "And yet, with equal advantages, they would be equal in capacity to ourselves!"

Yes! Equal to the British!

Then the questions began:

*"Do the slaves show great apprehension on being sold?"*

"They imagine they are being bought to be eaten," John answered. "You can imagine their terror."

*"Is the condition of the slaves that are not sold worse than that of the slave in our islands?"*

"It's true that the situation of slaves in Africa is bad," John conceded. "But it's even worse on board slave ships, and it's worst of all on our islands."

*But is the slave trade profitable?*

"Not to my employers," John answered. "There were gainful voyages, to be sure, but the losing voyages were more numerous. It was generally considered a sort of lottery in which every adventurer hoped to win a prize."

Considering his inside knowledge of the slave trade—including his admitted involvement in it—along with his respected reputation, John Newton's evidence carried a great deal of weight with the committee. In fact, before dismissing him, the council commended him for his final voyage on the *African* during which he had not lost a single crew member nor one enslaved African. "Not even an ordinary vessel could boast such a record!" one MP said. But praise for such an accomplishment while he was still pursuing a business "so iniquitous, so cruel, so oppressive, so destructive, as the African slave trade" deeply embarrassed the reformed sea captain, and he left the chamber most distressed.

Powerful pro-slavery members of Parliament lost no time in doing their best to rebut John's testimony. "Does he take us for fools?" several mocked. "Why would anyone in his right mind, whose profit depends on possessing healthy African natives, purposely torment and distress them during their voyage—much less *kill* them? That would be too absurd!"

Mainly, though, they hammered away on their central theme: to abolish the slave trade would topple the British economy. London, Liverpool, and Bristol would all be ruined. Other major cities, too. A rather effective argument, actually, considering that during the Atlantic trade, British ships made around 12,000 voyages and carried 2.6 million slaves. In 1797, one in every four ships leaving the port of Liverpool was a slaver. In fact, Liverpool alone handled over half of Europe's slave trade.

Furthermore, the objectors insisted that without slave labor, Britain would certainly lose her colonies to other nations with less sensitive consciences. Why, merely entertaining such a discussion as this was certain to be interpreted as a sign of weakness that would surely lead to more slave revolts.

But armed with John Newton's testimony and his well-circulated writings, as well as evidence from others, William Wilberforce replied, "Is it right that our contentment be dependent on the misery of people in another part of the world?" The important issue for Britain, he insisted, was not what was expedient, but what was right.

Back at home, John assured Mary all was well. It was not a battle that would be easily won, he said. And although it was late and he was exhausted, John could not sleep. Instead, he picked up his Olney hymnal and, alone in the parlor, he leafed through it. When he got to hymn number 41, he stopped and carefully read again his own story:

> Amazing grace! (how sweet the sound)
>     That sav'd a wretch like me!
> I once was lost, but now am found,
>     Was blind, but now I see.

> 'Twas grace that taught my heart to fear,
>     And grace my fears reliev'd;
> How precious did that grace appear,
>     The hour I first believ'd!

> Thro' many dangers, toils and snares,
>     I have already come;
> 'Tis grace has brought me safe thus far,
>     And grace will lead me home.

Any hesitation John had continued to feel about speaking from the pulpit against the injustice of the slave trade was gone. Just as God had given William Wilberforce a platform, he had also given one to John. And just as John was challenging Wilberforce to make the most of the position in which God had placed him, John Newton determined anew not to waste a single moment of the time and place God had set before him. "I hope, and I believe, that a very great majority of the nation earnestly longs for the suppression of slavery," he proclaimed. "But hitherto, petty and partial interests prevail against the voice of justice, humanity, and truth."

Well, that was changing fast. Within months of John's testimony, Thomas Clarkson built a model of the slave ship the *Brookes*, fully loaded with 482 slaves. Produced as posters, copies of this shocking reproduction were distributed throughout Britain to a horrified public. It was one thing to hear rumors and statistics— even descriptions—but quite another to see an actual model laid out in appalling detail.

But Mary's illness was advancing. Soon she was no longer able to move from her bed. To John in his sadness she simply said, "I still have the use of my hands. I'm very thankful for that." The time came, however, when she could not even bear the sound of the softest footsteps on the carpet, nor the gentlest voices whispering around her.

On Sunday, December 15, 1790, while John was preparing to give the morning's sermon, Mary sent for him to say a final good-bye. Gently John took the hands of his wife—his Polly—his dearest—the woman he had loved for most of his life—and he wept. "Are you in a state of peace, my dearest?" he whispered, knowing full well she could no longer speak. "If so, hold up your hand." Not only did Mary hold up her hand, but she waved it back and forth, and back and forth, and back and forth.

The moment John finished his sermon, he hurried back to sit by Mary's bedside. Winter darkness shrouded the room, so he lit a candle and continued to sit long into the night. He was beside her when she breathed her last. Mary—vibrantly fun-loving. Mary—who provided exactly the balance John needed in his life. Mary—who loved nothing so much as digging in her garden, who could talk for hours to William Cowper about geraniums and cucumbers and melons. Mary—who skipped happily through the outdoors with Betsy, telling her it was but a memory of Paradise. Mary—who John had loved since the day he first saw her, a girl of fourteen. Mary—his dearest, the love of his life, was now in heaven.

"Every room where you're not present looks unfurnished," John lamented aloud as he walked though their house. And he told his closest friends, "Her image follows me in every room." Some wondered if he and Betsy would leave the house in Charles Square, but it was their home, and there they remained.

John Newton's fame had spread across the ocean to the fledgling country known as the United States of America—where he had come so close to moving. In 1790, the University of New Jersey conferred upon him the honorary degree of Doctor of Divinity. Along with the diploma, he received a work in two volumes dedicated to him with the degree letters D.D. added to his name.

What an honor! But, no. . . . In grateful acknowledgement, John declined. "I am as one born out of due time," he wrote. "I have neither the pretension nor wish to honors of this kind. The dreary coast of Africa was the university to which the Lord was pleased to send me, and I dare not acknowledge a relation to any other." Even so, admirers in Scotland insisted on sending him letters addressed to Dr. John Newton. John sent them back marked, "I know of no such person."

Finally, in 1791, William Wilberforce was able to formally introduce a bill for the abolition of slavery. He stood before Parliament and cried, "Africa, Africa, your sufferings have been the theme that has arrested and engages a heart. Your sufferings no tongue can express, no language impart." After three hours of debates in which opponents did their best to discredit the bill, Wilberforce concluded with, "You may choose to look the other way, but you can never again say you did not know."

The bill was easily defeated by a vote of 163 to 88.

✦

When St. Mary Woolnoth Church was closed for repairs later that year, John and Betsy left London for four months. The still-popular minister had invitations to preach in the surrounding area, and the time away gave them a chance to visit with friends. One July morning, the two walked together along the beach at Dover. "What a wretch I was," John said, shaking his head as he remembered the last time he was in that spot. It was 1745 and he was just twenty years old. "What misery lay before me! But oh, what mercy and good God has shown to me since that day!"

In Southampton, where he so often went with Mary, John wrote in his journal, "Looks like a weeping day. It rains much and in the garden seems to drop tears upon me as I pass along. I miss my dear in every room and on every walk."

Twice he stood in his old pulpit in Olney and preached, just as if time had never passed. Only now, Mary was not there.

John observed the first anniversary of Mary's death at home by himself, praying and praising God for the years they had together. "I have been able to live a year without her, though she is always in my mind," he wrote. And even though Mary wasn't there, home was still a loving and pleasant place to be. Betsy made it so.

✦

The American Revolution had been a time of great turmoil, and although John prayed regularly for God's will in those fearful times, and though he had repeatedly said prayers from the pulpit, he always wished he had organized regular prayer. Now another awful period had begun—this time in France—and it was tearing Europe apart. John helped establish regular prayer meetings at the start of the French Revolution and they continued until the end in 1795.

As for the slave trade, it was never far from his mind or his lips. "I regard it not as a political, but as a moral view," he told any who commented about his sermons on the subject. In 1792, when William Wilberforce renewed his motion in the House of Commons for the abolition of the slave trade, Mr. Newton preached on the subject with renewed passion, just as he had when the bill was proposed the previous year. By that time, nearly half a million British citizens had signed petitions to end the trade. Some states in America also banned slave trading. And yet, the abolitionists were defeated again and again. Even a resolution to gradually abolish the trade fell to defeat in the House of Lords.

"Perhaps I'm not the one to lead this fight," a discouraged Wilberforce said to John. "Look at the opposition! The Duke of Clarence—our next king!—with the support of his father, insisted he has proof that the slaves are not, as a rule, treated in the way you said, and that you describe in your writing. He painted an entirely different picture—one of slaves in a state of humble happiness. Yes, happiness! And Lord Barrington . . . he went so far as to claim that slaves appeared to him so happy that he often *wished himself to be in their situation!*"

At that, John laughed out loud. "My dear lad," he said, "I can only say that I wish he were in their situation, too!" Then he said,

"William, Lord Barrington is heir to a merchant trader. The slave trade means a great deal of money to him. And as for the Duke of Clarence . . . really, now . . . what does he know about anything?"

Now it was Wilberforce's turn to laugh.

"I stayed in the trade far too long," John said. "People always ask me why. Well, it was acceptable and legal, and it did have immediate and tangible benefits. Furthermore, people then as now predicted widespread calamity should it ever be banned. At that time, there was no social pressure against it to cause me any shame. Yes, the fight is hard. And it will continue to be hard, precisely because the slaving interests are so well represented in Parliament. But take heart. Right will prevail!"

# CHAPTER 22

# 1797

*"Oh, it was mercy indeed to save a wretch like me!"*

"BETSY, MY DEAR," JOHN SAID EAGERLY, HANDING HER THE NEW BOOK just delivered to him, "can you read some of this to me?" His eyesight, always poor, was now failing badly, which caused him no end of frustration. Reading and writing letters—two of his greatest joys—had become next to impossible.

The book Betsy began reading that day was William Wilberforce's newly published, *The Practical View of Religion*. So intrigued was her beloved uncle that she read on and on into the night. When she finally came to the end, Newton exclaimed, "This book *must* and *will* be read by many in the higher circles—people to whom we little folks can get no access. If we preach, they will not hear us. If we write, they will not read. But they will read this!"

Times were hard, and much was happening to keep lawmakers distracted from the plight of African slaves. Rather than coming to an end, the awful wars of the French Revolution merged into even more dangerous wars as Napoleon Bonaparte rose up and took over the French revolutionary government. Britain found itself beset by naval defeat, by mutiny, and by repeated attempts by the French to invade its land.

John never lost interest in William Cowper, who was gaining real notice in Britain's literary circles. In 1798, Betsy brought him a letter from his old friend, and John asked her to read it to him. It was a sad, melancholy message that began, "Adieu, dear friend. . . ." That was the last John heard from Cowper until his death. John Newton preached the funeral service for the troubled, brilliant man who through the years proved to be his most intimate friend.

"My legs, eyes, and ears all admonish me that I am growing old," John said with a sigh. That wasn't all: his memory was also failing. Even so, he continued to preach. And, amazingly, John seldom forgot anything while he was in the pulpit.

Still, time was exacting its toll. His dear Mary, gone. His father, long gone. Sweet Eliza, gone. The only family he had left was Betsy, and she meant everything to him. Every summer they went on a holiday trip together, and now that he was growing more feeble and could hardly see, he found himself depending on her more and more. She was always at his side.

Then in 1801, Betsy suddenly sank into what seemed to be a dark depression. When she continued to worsen, John took her to Reading so that she could be under the care of a doctor he knew to be especially competent. But Betsy refused to take her medicines, and she continued to sink further into despair. "Mental breakdown." That's how the doctor described her condition to John.

"Please, please heal my Betsy," John pleaded with God. Even so, he ended every prayer with, "But your will be done. She is your child."

Beside himself with distress as he watched Betsy grow worse, John contacted his many friends and implored them to pray. Still the girl worsened until she was quite deranged—quiet and sweet, and able to pay some attention to what was going on around her, but deranged nevertheless. And although she was perfectly healthy physically, Betsy was convinced that she would die at any moment.

"I'm sorry," the doctor finally told John. "I have no choice but to confine your niece to Bethlehem Hospital.

John staggered in horror. The notorious "Bedlam" Hospital for the insane? No! Not his sweet Betsy! But the doctor was insistent. John begged his friends, "Collect all the prayers for us that you can."

Every day, whether sunny or snowing, sun-drenched or biting cold, feeble John slowly shuffled to the hospital grounds, accompanied by one friend or another. He cringed as the inmates' hopeless moans assaulted his ears, and anguished screams echoing through the cracked windows tore at his heart. John always arrived at the precise hour on which he and Betsy had agreed. Even with his dimmed sight, he was able to pick out the window on the stark stone wall that opened into her cell. Pointing it out to his companion, John would eagerly ask, "Do you see a white handkerchief waving to and fro?" As soon as he was told, yes, the handkerchief was there, John sighed with relief. His Betsy had made it through another day. Slowly he shuffled back home to pray and wait for her healing and release.

Of all the things John Newton endured during his long life, Betsy's illness was the one that came closest to overwhelming him. "I never saw a man so cut up," said his friend Mr. Bull after he accompanied John to the hospital one day. "He is broken-hearted." But gradually Betsy began to recover. After a year, she was released from the horrendous hospital. In that entire year, John had never missed a single day in coming to check on her, nor had Betsy missed a day signaling him from her window.

In the beauty of summer's end, 1802, Betsy was sufficiently recovered to take a trip with John out to the country they so loved. She spent her time resting, walking in the quiet woods, and basking in the love and fawning attention of friends with John always near her side. And more quickly than anyone expected, Betsy recovered completely.

◆

The French Revolution and Napoleon were fast changing the face of Europe. Already the American Revolution had changed Britain. In fact, after the loss of the American colonies, some Englishmen began to look to the abolition of slavery as a means to redeem their nation. Even so, the long, hard battle against slavery was by no means won.

John Newton, however, was growing old and weary. Nearly eighty and almost completely blind—he was too deaf to really participate in a conversation—he still continued to preach. "The church is to be an equipping station and a mobilizer to send people into the culture to make a difference," he insisted.

Whenever someone asked him (as people frequently would), "How are you today?" John always smiled and answered, "I am just as God would have me be."

In 1802, Britain made peace with Napoleon at Amiens. But when that peace broke down, Napoleon renewed his plans to invade Britain. He almost certainly would have succeeded, too, except for a decisive British naval victory the following year—at Trafalgar under Horatio Nelson. All of Britain rejoiced.

When John turned eighty, caring friends feared that perhaps he was continuing his public ministry too long. "Might it not be best to consider your work done, and stop before you discover you can speak no longer?" they gently suggested.

"What!" John fairly shouted. "Shall the old African blasphemer stop while he can still speak?"

No one made such a suggestion again. Instead, every Sunday, Alderman Lea sent his carriage to take John to church. But the old man had grown so feeble—and so heavy!—that he needed to be lifted in and out of the coach. Still he was as capable as ever of preaching, though he could no longer see to read his text. His memory sometimes failed him, as did his voice on occasion, yet people insisted he had never been more collected and lively in the pulpit. Certainly he was every bit as popular as ever. People still crowded the church each week to hear him speak.

To John's great joy, Betsy, who had recovered totally, married a wonderful husband. The newlyweds made their home with John.

John Newton, rector of St. Mary Woolnoth Church for twenty-eight years, last preached from the pulpit in October 1806, when he spoke for the benefit of those suffering from the Battle of Trafalgar. But during his sermon, his memory slipped and he needed to be reminded of the subject of his talk. After that he didn't preach again. He did, however, sit in the pulpit where he could hear the curate speaking. He was too deaf to hear from the pews.

On March 25, 1805, the House of Commons passed a bill that made it unlawful for any British subject to transport slaves, but the House of Lords blocked the bill. The battle looked hopeless. The following year, however, Lord Grenville formed a Whig administration more friendly to such legislation. Both Grenville and his foreign secretary, Charles Fox, strongly opposed the slave trade. Fox and Wilberforce joined together to lead the abolition campaign in the House of Commons, while Grenville took up the task of persuading the House of Lords to accept the measure.

The following year, the bill was again brought before Parliament—to fiercely renewed opposition from slavery profiteers, and even a plea for more time from the Duke of Clarence (which moved Wilberforce to write to a friend, "It was truly humiliating to see, in the House of Lords, four of the royal family come down to vote against the poor, helpless, friendless slaves").

When the vote was taken, the bill sailed through the House of Commons 114 to 15, and it passed in the House of Lords by a vote of 41 to 20. As tears flooded Wilberforce's eyes and ran down his cheeks, the chamber erupted in three rousing cheers. In spite of his tears, Wilberforce laughed out loud! King George III gave his assent, and on March 25, 1807, it was now illegal to transport slaves into or out of England or any British territory. At long last, trading in slaves was essentially against the law throughout the British Empire.

When William Wilberforce came to give his dear mentor the good news, John Newton congratulated him heartily, then he expressed his own gratitude for the great moral victory Wilberforce had won for the nation.

"But I couldn't have done it without you," Wilberforce told John. "You did so much to help change the hearts and minds of the people of Britain. In a way, it was you who provided our nation with an opportunity for redemption."

John tried to brush off Wilberforce's words. But William, leaning forward to make certain the old man heard him, said, "I think that although your testimony before Parliament was your own test of faith, the effect of your words changed hearts and minds on that day." Then he added, "Even more were changed by your example."

John grasped the hand of the man who had become so dear to him, and with all his strength, he squeezed it. "My memory is nearly gone," he said, "but I can remember two things: that I am a great sinner, and that Christ is a great Savior!"

That evening, after William Wilberforce left, John Newton took paper and pen and wrote out his congratulations:

"Although I can scarcely see the paper before me, I must attempt to express my thankfulness to the Lord, and to offer my congratulations to you, for the success which he has so far been pleased to give to your unwearied endeavors for the abolition of the slave trade, which I have considered a millstone, sufficient—of itself sufficient—to sink such an enlightened and highly favored nation as ours to the bottom of the sea."

It had long been John Newton's deepest prayer that God would allow him to live long enough to see the slave trade outlawed in Britain, and he spent an entire day giving thanks for the answer to that prayer. No longer could he read the words to *Amazing Grace*. It didn't matter. Each one was forever etched on his heart as was the tune of the lament that long-ago nameless Africans cried out from deep in the hold of the slave ship. John couldn't read the Scriptures any more, either, but over the years he had memorized so much of it that despite his fading memory, the precious words came back to him at just the right time: "What does the Lord require of you but to do justly, to love mercy, and to walk humbly with your God?" (Micah 6:8). His physical eyes were all but useless, yet never had he seen the truth of God's grace more clearly. "I once was blind," John Newton whispered with a smile, "but now . . . oh, now I truly see!"

By terms of the new law, any British captain caught carrying slaves was fined one hundred pounds for every African captive found on board his ship. The blight of slave trafficking didn't simply disappear, however. Not a practice as lucrative and well-entrenched as the slave trade. Slave ship captains who feared their vessels were in danger of capture by the British navy simply cut their losses by throwing the Africans overboard and drowning the evidence. Also, slavery itself remained legal in Britain and its colonies until 1838, and in America until 1865.

As the seasons changed and the days grew short, John was completely confined to his bed. One evening he said to Betsy, "When I shut my eyes on the things of time, I shall open them in a better world. What a thing it is to live under the shadow of the wings of the Almighty!"

"The Lord is gracious," Betsy replied.

John answered, "If it were not so, how could I dare to stand before him?"

> The Lord has promis'd good to me,
>> His word my hope secures;
> He will my shield and portion be,
>> As long as life endures.

> Yes, when this flesh and heart shall fail,
>> And mortal life shall cease;
> I shall possess, within the vail,
>> A life of joy and peace.

Surely John would have fully embraced the final verse of his hymn, taken from the anonymous *O Jerusalem, My Happy Home* and already added to *Amazing Grace* in America:

> When we've been there ten thousand years,
>> Bright shining as the sun,
> We've no less days to sing God's praise
>> Than when we'd first begun.

On December 12, 1807—in his eighty-third year—John Newton died peacefully at home, his loving Betsy at his side. At his funeral, over thirty ministers of various denominations—men who normally could hardly abide each other's presence—sat side by side and paid tribute to the man who was able to bridge divides as none of the rest of them could.

Since John Newton knew exactly how he wanted to be remembered, long before he needed it, he wrote out a final inscription for his grave marker, along with the instructions that it be inscribed on a plain marble tablet, and that he be buried next to his dear Mary in a grave beside St. Mary Woolnoth Church. Absolutely no monument was to be added. And nothing should be included on the marker but his own words:

John Newton,
CLERK,

ONCE AN INFIDEL AND LIBERTINE,
A SERVANT OF SLAVES IN AFRICA,
WAS,
BY THE RICH MERCY OF OUR LORD AND SAVIOUR

JESUS CHRIST,

PRESERVED, RESTORED, PARDONED,
AND APPOINTED TO PREACH THE FAITH
HE HAD LONG LABOURED TO DESTROY.

------------

HE MINISTERED
NEAR XVI YEARS AS CURATE AND VICAR
OF OLNEY IN BUCKS,
AND XXVIII, AS RECTOR
OF THESE UNITED PARISHES.

-------------

ON FEBRUARY, THE FIRST MDCCL HE MARRIED
MARY,
DAUGHTER OF THE LATE GEORGE CATLETT,
OF CHATHAM, KENT,
WHOM HE RESIGNED TO THE LORD WHO GAVE HER,
ON DECEMBER THE XVTH, MDCCXC.

In 1893, when all grave sites were removed from the yard beside St. Mary Woolnoth Church, John and Mary Newton were re-interred beside the church in Olney.

It wasn't until twenty-four years later after John's death, as William Wilberforce was dying, that he finally received the news: at long last Parliament had abolished slavery in Britain and all its territories. One by one, other nations followed. Yet it wasn't until 1962 that slavery was finally made illegal throughout the world.

"Perhaps what I have said of myself will be applicable to the nation at large," John Newton wrote in *Thoughts on African Slave Trade*. "The slave trade was always unjustifiable, but inattention and interest prevented for a time the evil from being perceived."

Yes. Even applicable in the twenty-first century, it would seem.

"It is no longer so." John wrote.

Let us pray to that end.

# EPILOGUE

*"You may choose to look the other way, but you can never again say you did not know."*
~*William Wilberforce*~

SLAVERY. A CURSE ON SOCIETY. SINFUL AND DEHUMANIZING. THANK God those days are behind us. After so long, we have finally moved beyond treating human beings as objects to be owned and used and abused. Right?

Think again. Today, two hundred years after John Newton struggled alongside William Wilberforce to bring an end to the African slave trade, three times as many people around the world are living as slaves. When the first abolition bill passed in 1807, four million people were enslaved; today the number is more like twelve million.[1]

"But, the law. . . ."

Ah, yes. The law. Well, as Lord Shelbourne—prime minister of Britain before William Pitt—said, "It requires no small labor to open the eyes of either the public or of individuals. . . . But real difficulty remains in getting people to apply the principles which they have admitted and are convinced."

Today, we all know slavery is wrong. It's illegal in every country

---

1. UNICEF, 2003.

of the world. In 1948, the United Nations condemned it in the Universal Declaration of Human Rights, then reaffirmed that condemnation in 1956 with a supplemental act. But those who cannot read and write don't understand the laws. Exploited children are powerless. No one listens to the cries of the destitute. So they will continue to suffer unless we who do understand, and who have power and influence, insist that the existing laws be enforced on their behalf.

The thing is, slavers today don't sail the high seas with chained captives packed into the holds of their ships. And they certainly don't march the slaves out to auction blocks behind the post office and sell them to the highest bidder. They don't even use the word "slave." Yet when people are owned as property, bought and sold, physically punished for not working hard enough, locked up so they can't leave, and thrust into deplorable or dehumanizing work conditions, then, whatever they're called, they are slaves.

And by whatever name—sex trafficking, bonded labor, child labor—slavery still wears the individual faces of personal suffering:

- *Vera, a skinny thirteen-year-old with long brown hair and little-girl bangs, was kidnapped by her neighbor in Albania. He whisked her out of the country and sold her into prostitution.* Forcing a woman or girl into commercial sex—especially one under eighteen—is one of the most common forms of slavery trafficking today. Sex trafficking is rampant around the world—especially in eastern Europe, Asia, India, Nepal.

- *Every day, from dawn until dark, Kumar labors in his land-owner's fields, his wife and ten-year-old son working by his side. Even so, his debt is greater today than when he inherited it from his father.* Millions of people are enslaved as bonded laborers, especially in India—particularly Dalits, members of the untouchable caste. Their enslavement comes with a moneylender's loan, even just the few rupees it costs to buy medicine for a sick child. Laborers must work long hours in the fields or the factory or the rock quarry seven days a week, and they must accept the moneylender's meager shelter and food, which is added to their bill at an inflated price. Regardless of how long or how hard they work, the debt may never be paid off. Some families are enslaved for generations.

- *Little Ricardo works in Ecuador's banana fields seven days a week. He doesn't even dream of school. No one he knows can read or write. Nor does he hope for a future. What meaning does "hope" or "future" have for him?* Cheap, and unlikely to either complain or demand, children work long hours in agriculture and factories around the world. Besides keeping them out of school—if school is even available—their jobs are often harmful to their health and well-being. About 218 million children between the ages of five and seventeen are trapped in child labor, according to the International Labor Organization (ILO).

- *In Uganda, ten-year-old Jackson was on his way to school when he was abducted at gunpoint and forced to become a soldier for the notorious Lord's Resistance Army (LRA). He has seen—and done—things too awful to speak about.* As many of the 300,000 child soldiers are forced into over thirty areas of conflict around the world. About 80 percent of the LRA ranks are child abductees—some as young as eight years old. Most of these children suffer severe trauma and guilt and terror. How could it be otherwise?

- *A slave? Nona, the Long Island couple's Indonesian maid? Who would have guessed the woman who brought the trash out to the curb each week was being beaten, starved, and scalded with boiling water? Locked in the basement and forced to work without pay? Nona was the victim of a "bait-and-switch" employment scheme.* Yes, slaves can be found even in such places as New York, London, and Toronto. Similar to "bonded laborers," workers are brought to the U.S., Britain, or Canada, then tricked into working for little or no pay. Domestic and sex workers are trafficked in with promises of jobs or education. The U.S. government estimates that between 15,000 and 18,000 are trafficked into America each year.

Never have we needed John Newton's legacy more than today! The call to end slavery in the 1700s was quite remarkable, really: white Britons demanding justice for black Africans on the other side of the word, people they didn't know and with whom they had not the least bit in common. Never before had people became so incensed over the misery of others unlike themselves that they surged to action and demanded change.

Today we passionately champion many causes of injustice and suffering, however, not necessarily slavery. Most people think that it is a thing of the past, so they fix their sights on other causes, which is exactly what traffickers would like to see continue. For if we remain blind to the problem, we won't become incensed. Then we won't surge to action and demand change.

## How You Can Be a Twenty-first Century Abolitionist:

So, now what? How can we be effective abolitionists in our time?

Well, it is indeed a complex problem, even more so than in John Newton's day. Some of the things that seem obvious, such as boycotting products and crops produced under terrible conditions, actually hurt the oppressed workers more than they hurt those perpetrating the oppression. Rather than an *action*, today's abolition is a *process*. People with legal knowledge and abilities, and with global expertise, are already at work. (See appendix 1 for a list of active organizations.) But they cannot get the job done alone.

Here are some steps you can take:

- **Support organizations that are in a position to make a difference.** Most of those listed in appendix 1 depend upon donations. Contributing to them will allow them to continue to do what they do best.

- **Educate yourself, then pass your knowledge on.** Read the websites of the organizations listed. When they offer further information, take them up on it. Become a slavery expert. Then write or speak or pass on materials. Do whatever you can to educate those around you.

- **Join a group.** Let it keep you up-to-date on what's happening in the fight against slavery as well as where you might be able to help. And don't underestimate the power of the church. As John Newton said, "Church is to be an equipping station and a mobilizer to send people to the culture to make a difference." Let's do it!

- **Make your voice heard.** Your elected officials need to know how vital this issue is to you. Petition them to place a high priority on enforcing anti-slavery laws, and to put real pressure on countries that tolerate forced labor.

- **Buy fairly traded products.** The fair trade program provides a sustainable model of international trade based on economic justice. (To find out more, see www.fairtrade.net.) Many major supermarkets sell fair trade products, as do a number of catalog-order companies. If your local retailer doesn't stock them, write and ask that they do so.

- **Step into the gap on another's behalf.** If you suspect someone is being coerced or held against his or her will, call the U.S. Department of Justice toll free hotline: 1-888-428-7581. In the U.K. the confidential number is: 0800-555-111. All you need do is place the call. The professionals will take it from there.

- **Pray.** Micah 6:8 says, "What does the Lord require of you but to do justly, to love mercy, and to walk humbly with your God?" Ask God for the ability and wisdom to do all three.

Imagine if we resolved to never look away from the plight of those who are enslaved today.

Imagine if we became so incensed over what is already illegal that we refused to allow it to exist.

Imagine if we saw slavery ended in our day!

# APPENDIX 1

The following organizations are actively involved in the global fight to end slavery. Any or all are eager to have your help!

**Anti-Slavery International**
Thomas Clarkson House
The Stableyard, Broomgrove Road
London SW9 9TL
United Kingdom
Tel: 44(0)20 7501 8920
Contact: info@antislavery.org
Website: www.antislavery.org

This organization lobbies governments, supports research, educates the public on slavery, and runs rehabilitation and liberation projects.

## Clear International

The Ship
Ship Lane
Marsworth, Bucks HP23 4NA
United Kingdom
Contact: international@lawcf.org
Website: www.clearinternational.org

Using local lawyers, this grass roots organization seeks redress in individual cases of injustice in the developing world through the local justice system.

## Free the Slaves

1012 14th St. NW Ste. 600
Washington, D.C. 20005
United States of America
Tel: (202) 638-1865
Contact: info@freetheslaves.net
Website: www.WarSlavery.org

A nonprofit organization dedicated to ending slavery around the world, Free the Slaves works toward this end with partner organizations, conducts research, and encourages others to take action in the anti-slave movement.

## International Justice Mission

P.O. Box 58147
Washington, D.C. 20037-8147
United States of America
Tel: (703) 536-3730
Contact: ijm@ix.netcom.com
Website: www.ijim.org

A human rights agency that rescues victims of violence, sexual exploitation, slavery, and oppression, IJM began operations after a group of human rights professionals, lawyers, and public officials launched an extensive study of the injustices witnessed by overseas relief and development workers.

**Operation Mobilization**
 PO Box 660
 Forest Hill
 London Hill
 London SE23 3ST
 United Kingdom
 Tel: 0208-8699-6077
 Website: http://www.om.org/general.jsp (contains links to websites around the world)

Using a variety of approaches, Operation Mobilization works in more than a hundred countries to motivate and equip people to share God's love with others all over the world, especially in areas where Christ is least known.

**PROGRESS**
 12-13-623 Tarnaka
 Hyderabad –17
 India
 Tel: 91-08415-22069

This progressive organization makes use of the expertise of top scientists who explore cutting-edge possibilities for using technologies to change the plight of India's poor and downtrodden. The result has been astounding strides in the area of micro-enterprise.

**The Salvation Army**

International Headquarters
101 Queen Victoria St
London EC4P 4EP
United Kingdom
Tel: (020) 7332 0101
Tel: [44] (20) 7332 0101 (international)
Website: http://www.salvationarmy.org
(This site has links to the trafficking division, and also to the following major English language websites: Australia, Canada, New Zealand, the United Kingdom, and the United States of America. In addition a drop-down list of numerous other country choices is available.)

The anti-trafficking office of this well-known and respected organization develops services for trafficking victims and presses for greater local church involvement and public policy reform.

**TearFund UK**

100 Church Road
Teddington, Middlesex TW11 8QE
United Kingdom
Contact: enquiry@tearfund.org
Website: www.tearfund.org

One of the United Kingdom's leading relief and development charities, TearFund has local partnerships in seventy countries. A founding member of the Stop the Traffic coalition calling for an end to people trafficking, this organization is committed to offering hope, providing a meaningful future, and speaking out against injustice.

## World Relief

7 E. Baltimore St.
Baltimore, Maryland 21202
United States of America
Tel: (800) 535-LIFE
Website: www.worldrelief.org

Originated within the National Association of Evangelicals, World Relief works around the world through Faith Alliance Against Slavery and Trafficking (FAAST) International, a network of faith-based organizations that combat trafficking (www.faastinternational.org).

## World Vision International

800 West Chestnut Avenue
Monrovia, California 91016-3198
United States of America
Tel: (626) 303-8811
Website: http://www.wvi.org (links to regional offices throughout the world)

A Christian organization, World Vision International is dedicated to ending poverty, hunger, and human rights abuses worldwide.

# APPENDIX 2

Bohrer, Dick (paraphrased). *John Newton, Letters of a Slave Trader Freed by God's Grace.* Moody: Chicago, 1983.

Bull, Josiah. *"But Now I See": The Life of John Newton.* Banner of Truth Trust: Edinburgh, 1868.

Newton, John (intro by Bruce Hindmarsh). *The Life and Spirituality of John Newton.* Regent College Pub: Canada, 1998.

Newton, John (intro by Herbert Lockyer). *Out of the Depths: An Autobiography.* Kregel Publications: Grand Rapids, 1990. (first published as letters in 1764)

Newton, John. *Thoughts Upon the African Slave Trade.*

Strom, Kay Marshall. *John Newton: The Angry Sailor.* Moody: Chicago, 1984.